EILEEN GEORGE'S

CONVERSATIONS IN HEAVEN III

To Jessy,

Love & Peace
Eileen George
A.M.D.G.

Other Eileen George Books:

Eileen George: Beacon of God's Love: Her Teaching

Eileen George's *Conversations in Heaven I*
Dialogues with Jesus and God the Father

Eileen George's *Conversations in Heaven II*

For ordering information, see last page

EILEEN GEORGE'S

CONVERSATIONS IN HEAVEN

III

THE MEET-THE-FATHER MINISTRY, Inc.
363 Greenwood St.
Millbury, MA 01527

Library of Congress Catalog Card Number 96-76537

ISBN 0-9624588-4-8 Volume Three 10.00

Published with ecclesiastical permission

Ecclesiastical permission is not a judgment that the contents of the book are of supernatural origin.

363 Greenwood St.
Millbury, Mass. 01527

Printed in the United States of America

First Edition
1996

TABLE OF CONTENTS

PART FOUR: REVEALING HEAVEN

EPILOGUE

INDEX

PHOTOGRAPHS

After PART TWO

FOREWORD

EILEEN GEORGE'S MESSAGE

The message of Eileen George is both manifold and simple. **In her services, audio and visual tapes and in her book** *Eileen George: Beacon of God's Love: Her Teaching*, her message is the unconditional, infinite, tender love of the Father for all His children. Eileen explains that the way to the Father is through "falling in love" with Jesus. The way to falling in love with Jesus is through spending "love-time" with Him, through reading about Him in the Scriptures, through uniting oneself with Him in the Sacrament of Reconciliation "which opens the spiritual taste buds of the soul" and through the ecstasy of union with Him in His Eucharistic sacrifice and in Communion. The proof that there is "no hole in the bucket" through which these precious graces are lost, is that we become better people, better wives and husbands, fathers and mothers, children, better citizens, and that we hold no grievances but are reconciled with those with whom we are estranged. "Call your mother-in-law and tell her you love her and you want to have dinner with her."

If we are humble we will accept the teaching and discipline of the Church and follow the example of the Savior. We will avoid gossip, especially about priests: "We are to love them and not to judge them. God will judge them."

Besides her public teaching, we have **an insight into her private life.** This came about because after celebrating Mass for Eileen privately, her spiritual director taped her thanksgiving while she was in ecstasy. It became evident from her dialogues with Jesus and the Father that God wanted these conversations to become known. Therefore they have been published in the books *Conversations in Heaven I, II* and *III.* This book completes the series.

The *Conversations in Heaven* series lifts the curtain on Eileen's spiritual life, on her dialogues with Jesus and the Father. They also manifest the relations of the persons of the Trinity with each other and with Eileen, and reveal God's heavenly kingdom.

We believe the doctrine contained in Eileen's public teaching insofar as it is the doctrine of the Church. We accept what her conversations in Heaven reveal insofar as we accept the witness of Eileen and insofar as it is in accordance with the teaching of the Church. This comes easier to those who know Eileen through her services. For others it may be difficult. By them, these conversations may be accepted as a faith-filled meditation. Chapter One of *Eileen George: Beacon of God's Love: Her Teaching* is entitled "Eileen George's Credentials." Some of this material is also contained in the Foreword and in the Introduction of *Conversations in Heaven I.* A section of this Introduction is entitled "Is Heaven as Eileen Describes It Credible?"

The revelation of Heaven contained in the dialogue series may seem strange, even fantastic, because of the silence of theologians on this subject. This silence has been broken by Msgr. James O'Connor, among others, in his book *Land of the Living* (with a foreword by John Cardinal O'Connor). Msgr. O'Connor has taught theology for twenty years at St. Joseph's Seminary (Dunwoodie) in the Archdiocese of New York. His book draws on Catholic teaching from the early Church to the present.

In the early Church and even later a more descriptive account was given of Heaven than in recent centuries. St. Bernard, describing the joys of Heaven, said that all earth's beauties will be present so that God being seen in all creatures He may be praised (*Land of the Living,* page 185). Commenting on Romans 8:21, St. Chrysostom says: "What is this creation [that will be brought into the glorious freedom of the children of God]? Not only you but that which is inferior to you. That which does not share with you reason or sense perception will share with you the good things [to come] . . . It will no longer be corruptible, but will follow after the beauty of your body. As you were made corruptible so it was made corruptible. When you are made incorruptible so it too will follow." (page 174 – also for what follows). St. Augustine wrote of a new heaven and a new earth which would exist for the sake of beauty, a loveliness that would delight the mind and lead the saints to praise the Source of all beauty. There rest would not mean a cessation of motion, but motion would be an aspect of beauty. Put in what you want, he said, save corruption. His saying compares with that of St. Thomas that there is no imperfection in Heaven. Unfortunately St. Thomas was unable to reconcile motion, except what he considered to be the perfect motion of the planets, with perfection. Hence Heaven for him was like the moon: bereft of any adornment. His view prevailed until very recently.

The Teaching of Christ. A Catholic Catechism for Adults, first edition, while stating that "Heaven is more a state of being, a sharing of the divine life and joy, than a place," also says: "Nothing will be lost of all the precious things that were. In the resurrection the flesh of all whom we have loved will be restored; the new heavens and the new earth will guard all that has been precious in time." Such is the Heaven that appears in this book.

Hence we can understand that for Msgr. O'Connor the adornment of Heaven will be plants, such as flowers, and animals [the animals that we love]. The importance of filling out a description of Heaven, as Msgr. O'Connor explains, is that we are strongly moved to desire what is concrete and appealing.

Theologians speculate about what Scripture has not revealed. Eileen's revelations are significant, since that about which theologians speculate, she has seen and touched. This she witnesses to us through the recordings of her conversations in Heaven.

INTRODUCTION

I. ABOUT REVELATION

This Introduction is adapted for this book from the Introduction to *Conversations in Heaven I.* For those who do not have the first book of the series, this will permit this volume to be a standalone work. The nature of Eileen's conversations need an introduction, as will be obvious from what follows.

The Church is cautious about private revelations for good reason, but she knows that there are true prophets as well as false prophets. In addition, what requires special consideration is the fact that these conversations are presented as occurring in the place Eileen will occupy in Heaven, if she remains faithful. This place Eileen describes in detail. She visits other "plateaus of Heaven," including one reserved to angels. These revelations make Heaven and the Persons whose companionship she enjoys there better known. We hear Eileen speaking with Jesus, with the Father, and with the Holy Spirit. At times they ask her to repeat what they are saying. Then we hear their words, which are intended also for us. We are present at celebrations with the friends of Jesus and Eileen.

Outside of an authentic tradition, these are matters which will sound fanciful. Within such a tradition they still remain open to doubt. It is therefore important to listen to what Scripture, the Church, and its experts, have to say about revelation and prophecy in order to even consider the possibility of such happenings. Of course it is well known that God showed Teresa of Avila the place in hell she would occupy if she did not reform her life. And it is also well known that the Father spoke at great length to a canonized saint and doctor of the Church, St. Catherine of Siena. The conversations are published in the *Dialogues.*

The teaching of Scripture and the Church on the charism of revelations is coherent and clear. The question of Eileen George's credibility is discussed in Chapter One of the book *Eileen George: Beacon of God's Love: Her Teaching,* and is touched on here.

St. John of the Cross, a doctor of the Church with special competence in these matters, speaks of revelations with great force: "In giving us His Son, His only Word (for He possesses no other), He spoke everything at once . . . " He adds: "any person . . . desiring some vision or revelation would be guilty not only of foolish behavior but also of offending Him by not fixing His eyes entirely on Christ and by living with the desire of some other novelty." [1] To look outside of the Word for revelations is to dishonor the gift of God.

Similarly the *Constitution on Divine Revelation* of Vatican Council II says, "He Himself (Jesus Christ) . . . completed and perfected revelation . . . and no new public revelation is to be expected before the glorious manifestation of our Lord Jesus Christ" [at the end of time]. [4] *The Catechism of the Catholic Church* adds that therefore religions based on supposed new public revelations have a false foundation. [67] Public revelation, completed and perfected in Jesus Christ, is the substance of Christian faith. It is all we need.

St. John of the Cross is concerned with directing souls to union with Jesus, and desire of the extraordinary is a blind detour on the road to this union. There is a difference, however, between seeking the charismatic gifts for oneself, and seeking them for the upbuilding of the Church. To the Corinthians, who were "eager for spiritual powers," St. Paul said, "Aim to be rich in those that build up the community." And again, "Make love your aim; but be eager, too, for spiritual gifts, and especially for prophesying. Those who speak in a tongue speak to God . . . someone who prophesies speaks to other people, building them up, and giving them encouragement and reassurance . . . those who prophesy build up the community."[2] Prophecy and revelation and other charisms need to be sifted and discerned by the Church, the pillar of truth.[3]

Concerning the presence of the charismatic gifts in lay persons like Eileen, the Fathers of Vatican Council II in the *Constitution on the Church* tell us: "Christ is the great prophet . . . he fulfills this prophetic office not only by the hierarchy, . . . but also by the laity. He accordingly both establishes them as witnesses and provides them with the appreciation of faith (*sensus fidei*) and the grace of the word." [35] *The Decree on the Apostolate of Lay People* adds: "From the reception of these charisms, even the most ordinary ones, there arises for each of the faithful the right and duty of exercising them in the Church and in the world for the good of men and the development of the Church, of exercising them in the freedom of the Holy Spirit who 'breathes where he wills' (John 3:8), and at the same time in communion with his brothers in Christ, and with his pastors especially." [3]

Furthermore, in the *Decree on the Ministry and Life of Priests* the Council Fathers say: "While trying the spirits to see if they be of God, priests must discover with faith, recognize with joy, and foster with diligence the many and various charismatic gifts of the laity." [9]

Thus the Church makes her own the teaching of St. Paul, who goes so far as to say that the Church is built on apostles and prophets . "You are built upon the foundations of the apostles and prophets, and Christ Jesus himself is the cornerstone."[4] He adds: "to some his [Christ's] 'gift' was that they should be apostles; to some prophets; to some evangelists; to some pastors and teachers to knit God's holy people together . . . to build up the Body of Christ . . . " (Ephesians 4:11)

Prophets are those God chooses as His messengers to bring the revelation He made once and for all in Christ to the attention of the Church. Karl Rahner writes of the prophet: "He is the envoy of God . . . He proclaims a message which makes demands . . . The prophet is the 'bearer of revelation'. . . Jesus Christ is the great prophet, the absolute bringer of salvation. This does not mean that prophecy has simply ceased. But the only [true] prophets are those who strive to uphold his message in its purity, who attest that message and make it relevant to their day . . . charismatic prophecy in the Church helps to make the message of Jesus new, relevant and actual in each changing age."[5]

Prophecy then is a message from God. Father Bruce Vawter

explains in a section of the New Jerome Biblical Commentary entitled, *The Nature of Prophecy:* "By prophecy we understand not specifically or even principally the forecasting of the future . . . but rather the mediation and interpretation of the divine mind . . . Prophecy not only was, but still is, the word of God. If all Scripture is, in its own measure, the word of God, it is preeminently true of the prophecy in which God chose to speak directly with his people. It is . . . the living word of a living God . . . the prophetic word is power from God and the prophet is the instrument through which this word is transmitted."[6] Father Vawter adds that "true and false prophets abound not only in antiquity, in the Old Testament and New Testament, within and without the people of God, but also in later times . . . it is plain that God spoke to his people through such instruments as Francis of Assisi, Vincent Ferrer, Catherine of Siena, Bridget of Sweden, and others, often through experiences like those of the biblical prophets."[7]

Thus during the Jansenist heresy, a withering wind blowing through the Church and shriveling trust in the mercy of God, Christ gave St. Margaret Mary Alacoque (1647-1690) the revelation of His Sacred Heart. This revelation was made known by her spiritual director, the Blessed Claude de la Colombiere, S.J., calling to the attention of all the mercy and love of Christ.

And in the materialistic 19th century which no longer believed in miracles or Heaven, God sent His Mother who announced herself as the Immaculate Conception to 14 year old Bernadette (1844-1879) to establish a shrine at Lourdes where cures occur which cannot be explained by medical science. Then God showed His concern for mankind through revelations to three children at Fatima, May to October 1917, when a wave of militant atheism was about to sweep the world and carry away a third of it. This wave of unbelief, which has spread throughout the world, encouraged the already widespread rejection of the supernatural, nourishing seeds of doubt and atheism everywhere. It left in its wake a distorted form of liberalism which was imbibed by many of the intellectuals of the Church, and with them by many of the faithful. It is only recently that the devastation worked in the Communist countries and in the West has been clear for all to see.

Against this spirit of disbelief, God sent Our Lady to the children at Fatima to reveal forthcoming events and truths of faith and to establish devotion to her Immaculate Heart. God pointed to Mary's heart as a sure way to the Heart of His Son and to His own. To Mary He confided the peace of the world. The message of Our Lady of Fatima, the message of the Hebrew prophets and of the Gospel, repent and pray, was given to three uneducated children to transmit to an age which has been losing its sense of sin and self-control.

II. ABOUT EILEEN

In view of these examples of divine mercy exercised through revelations made to children, is it inconceivable that God has raised up Eileen George at this particular time to reveal the Father and His tender love and mercy; to remind the world and priests that we have access to the Father through Jesus; and that the way to the love of Jesus is through love of neighbor, fidelity to one's duties and through the sacraments of the Church? In our day the sacrament of Reconciliation has fallen into disuse in the Church, while Jesus' real presence and transforming action in the Eucharist is being pushed into the background. Today the family, too, is under attack. *The Decree on the Apostolate of Lay People* of Vatican Council II tells us that the laity has a "special and indispensable role in the mission of the Church. Indeed, the Church can never be without the lay apostolate; it is something that derives from the layman's very vocation as a Christian." [1] Is it not appropriate that the God who sent a repentant woman to bring the news of Christ's resurrection to the foundation stones of the Church, should choose as a preacher and example of His love a laywoman, wife and mother of eight; one especially devoted to the duties of her state of life and a model of family life; a woman devoted to prayer who generously accepts repeated trials and sufferings to obtain the graces of conversion and holiness for all and especially for priests? Does not our Western world need a powerful renewal? And who better than the Father can initiate it?

For more than fifty years sociologists have been reminding us that we are in a post-Christian era. A Harvard psychiatrist has noted that whereas previously the most common mental disorders were due to repression, now they are due to lack of impulse control. He sees this as a result of the weakness of the father in the family.[8] With the breakdown of the family, the development of the character of children is impaired. Hence they are an easy prey to sex, alcohol, drugs, incapacity to make commitments, violence, suicide, need for immediate gratification, and to the loss of control of their impulses. Children who have not suffered this impairment are subject nonetheless to the peer pressure of the others, who form the juvenile culture of today. "A community that allows a large number of young men [and women] to grow up in broken families . . . never acquiring any stable relationship to male authority, never acquiring any set of rational expectations about the future . . . that community asks for and gets chaos" said Daniel Patrick Moynihan, sociologist, professor at Harvard and U.S. Senator.[9]

III. THE REMEDY: GOD THE FATHER

Knowledge of and devotion to God the Father is a remedy for the rapid deterioration of the family and society. Crucial to the Church and the world today is the realization of the role of the Father and of the Trinity in human affairs and in the search for happiness. Walter Kasper, theologian and now bishop, has come to the same conclusion. It is the theme of his book *The God of Jesus Christ.*[10] Eileen's conversations reveal to us how lovable the Father is, and how He wishes to be a part of our lives. Eileen's hearers and readers recognize that she speaks from experience about the kingdom and about the Persons of the Trinity.

Believers need to cling firmly to the teaching of the Church, founded on public revelation, that is Scripture and Tradition, authentically interpreted by the Church's living teaching office.[11] This is the foundation of the believer's divine and Catholic faith. It is by this that private revelation is to be judged and not vice versa.

The value of private revelation, as Karl Rahner says, is that it can recall the Gospel message according to the needs of the time. It can enliven, renew and deepen faith when it is faltering and becoming confused. That is the purpose of Eileen's books.

The ecclesiastical permission to publish is not a judgment that the contents of the book are of supernatural origin.

What Eileen sees and experiences of the kingdom can excite in us a deeper faith, that our hearts and lives may be filled with the joy of the Messiah, that we may look forward more eagerly to the joys awaiting us in our heavenly home. Eileen's experiences become our experience. They draw us to love the divine Persons and to accept their unbounded love with simplicity.

Are these revelations about Heaven revealed for one group of people only? As all people are the beloved children of the Father, so the mysteries of His love are for all who will accept them, to encourage all to come to the Father so that there may be in His Son one flock and one shepherd.[12] The Father is close to, and working in all who have unselfish love.

Eileen remains herself while responding to the Persons of the Trinity. She adores, loves, argues, questions, jokes, and in the end, submits. Pert though she is, she refuses nothing that God asks of her. If Eileen is an independent and strong-willed person, above all, she has an abiding sense of her own nothingness, a dependence on grace, and gratitude for the least grace given her.

It seems correct to say that the divine light is given to the prophet to know hiden things, or ignored teachings, to be told the people of God for the building up of the Church. (Hence the prophet's "private" revelations are not strictly private. We call them "private" to distinguish it from "public revelation," which ended with the apostles.)

Eileen is not only a prophet. She is also an intimate friend of Jesus and the Father, the spouse of the one, the faithful loving daughter of the other. God cannot withhold revealing His secrets from His close friends. He is goodness itself. As St. Thomas says when explaining the reasons for the Incarnation, goodness desires to communicate itself.[13] Of Abraham God said, "Shall I conceal from Abraham what I am going to do?"[14] Of Moses: "Yahweh would talk to Moses face to face as a man talks to his friend."[15] Of David God said: "I took you from the pasture from following the sheep, to be leader of my people Israel; I have been with you wherever you went."[16] John leaned on the bosom of Jesus[17] and learned from Him His secrets.

At this time when the Father discloses to Eileen that His Church is in serious danger He speaks face to face with her. Where the prophet is in contact with God Himself, the source of the prophetic light, there is the highest degree of prophecy.[18] Because of the uniqueness of her mission, the Father gave Eileen His Son as a companion from her childhood, then as a spouse. It was to make Heaven known that He brought Eileen into His heavenly kingdom and revealed its secrets to her. Eileen knows Heaven as we know earth -- from being there.

Humility, trust, generosity, willingness to embrace the sufferings of the cross, and obedience are necessary for friendship with God. Human qualities – education, intelligence, special natural gifts – do not qualify a person for the divine friendship. Indeed, their absence makes it more clear that it is God who is living and working in His friend. Friendship with God is a matter of a mutual love, given, accepted and worked for perseveringly. Rare are they who could receive such divine favors as God has accorded Eileen without a secret pride which would alienate them from God, Who resists the proud, but inclines to the humble. Bishop Timothy J. Harrington, the retired bishop of Worcester who has known Eileen remains the unassuming person she has always been.

While God gives His favors to whom He will, He does so for the welfare of others also. Eileen's humility and love entice us to enter into a closer friendship with the Father and Jesus. The love which Eileen pours out on the divine Persons, she also gives freely to others. She wishes all to have the benefit of her unique experiences. The Father's repeated instructions to her to withdraw into silence and solitude have proven a difficult cross for her. Compliance means not being available for one-to-one help to people. This goes against the grain of her deeply rooted compassionate desire to reach out to and help people in distress. The Father wants her now to reach out to them by prayer and sacrifice. He wants her to follow her deep attraction to the silence and solitude in which she can hear His voice, converse with Him and her beloved Jesus, receive His communications, and thus be better prepared to deliver His messages in her services, that this may be her gift to others.

The charm of this book is in the tenderness of these conversational partners. No attempt has been made to eliminate the playfulness of Jesus and Eileen, both of whom have retained their childlike hearts, nor to disguise the humor of the Father. These are a revelation in themselves and bring us closer to the divine Persons. Eileen's mission is to bring us into a more intimate union with Jesus Christ and the Father – and all their children. By rereading this book, you will provide the opportunity for her mission to be accomplished.

IV. WHAT TO AVOID

The Father's message given through Eileen commends the way of faith and love. Through faith we are united to Christ. By meditation on the truths contained in our faith we assimilate His message and put our life in order. Faith leads us to the sacrament of Reconciliation with its emphasis on amendment of life and to the Eucharist, by which we are intimately united to Jesus.

Eileen did not choose the way she was led. It was only gradually that she realized this way was not for everyone, but was a privilege. Often Eileen wishes that everyone could see Heaven as she does. Instead the Father has provided us with Eileen's eyes with which to see Heaven.

Perseveringly she advises our Lord to show Himself to His priests and people that they may believe He is present in the Eucharist and in the tabernacle. Jesus denies that this will be the way to the conversion of priests or the world. He insists that it is by seeking a personal relationship with Himself in faith that conversion will come about. He points to the need for an ever increasing faith, a gift to be asked for, but also something that one must work for.

Priests and people are often attracted to the extraordinary in Eileen's life. They want to have a ministry like hers. They want to be in the forefront and attract the attention of crowds. Eileen moans that they do not know the price of such a ministry – the suffering, humiliations, persecutions that it brings, and through which it becomes fruitful. Eileen urges priests and people to be faithful to the duties of their state of life. For priests this means accepting and being faithful in love to the ministry given them by their Bishop. She recommends awareness of the great privilege which is theirs to celebrate Mass and to hear confessions and give absolution. She commends the power of the Word proclaimed in fidelity to the Scriptures, sound doctrine and tradition. She recommends obedience to the Church in its doctrine and discipline.

It was necessary to make a decision about Eileen's manner of addressing Jesus as "Butchie." This seems irreverent, and threatens to be an obstacle for many. To understand it one needs to recall that before the age of three the Father took Eileen in hand by giving her as a companion, playmate and teacher a child about two or three years older than herself, who grew up with her. This companion said to her, "Call me 'Butchie,' and I'll call you 'Slug.'" A few years later Eileen realized that Butchie was Jesus. From then on she reverenced Him as the Son of God, but she continued to call Him "Butchie." God's desire to be with us on familiar terms led the Son of God to the womb of the Virgin, to the Cross, and to the Host where He became our food and drink. After that, is it surprising that to this child of His, He is "Butchie"?

1. St. John of the Cross. *Ascent of Mount Carmel*, Ch. 22, No.3-7
2. 1 Corinthians 12-14
3. 1 Tim. 3:15
4. Ephesians 2:20. The footnote in the *New Jerusalem Bible* says the New (not the Old) Testament prophets are here referred to.
5. "Prophetism" by Karl Rahner in *The Encyclopedia of Theology*, edited by Karl Rahner, 1975
6. *The New Jerome Biblical Commentary*, 1990, 11:3, 4, 25, pp.186-187, 199-120
7. ibid., No.4
8. I asked a friend, a graduate of the Harvard program in community psychiatry, Rabbi Earl Grollman of Beth-El Temple, Belmont, MA, if he could supply the reference for this opinion. He said he could not, but that he agreed with it.
9. Quoted in *The Great Reckoning. How the World Will Change in the Depression of the 1990s*, James Dale Davidson and Lord William Rees-Mogg, Simon and Schuster. New York. 1991, pg.257
10. Walter Kasper, *The God of Jesus Christ*, Crossroads. 1983. This is an excellent theological treatise. While it is not written for specialists, it requires very close reading.
11. "It is clear, therefore, that in the supremely wise arrangement of God, sacred Tradition, sacred Scripture, and the Magisterium of the Church are so connected and associated that one of them cannot stand without the others." *Constitution on Divine Revelation*, [10].
12. John 10:16
13. St. Thomas, *Summa Theologiae*, III,1

14. Genesis 18:17
15. Exodus 33:11
16. 2 Samuel 7:8,9
17. John 13:25,26
18. *Summa Theologiae*, II.II. 174,3 "Still higher is that grade of prophecy when, awake or asleep, there appears the very guise of God himself [*in specie Dei*], as in Isaiah, "I saw the Lord sitting upon a throne.""

PART ONE: EILEEN'S VALLEY

ONLY THROUGH DEATH I LIVE

January 8, 1984

Does He mean He'll withdraw the Spirit in the Renewal, or the Spirit with His gifts? See, I've got to know all of this stuff. I've got to know what He's talking about, and I can't get it, Butchie..... But I can't come until my Father brings me here. You know that I can't just take off and come here, my Father has to call me..... No, I don't want you to tell Him to call me. I want him to call me when He's ready..... No, I don't want to stay, I just want to be in my Father's will..... For sure I do. You know that I'd rather be here with You forever..... I want to do my Father's will. I don't want to come sooner than He wants me to come..... *(laughs)* Mary's the intercessor..... You're funny *(laughs)*..... That's all right. You can ask Him all You want. I'm not asking Him..... No..... He'll know when I'm ready.

At times I feel like – not that I'm ready. Not that I've reached where He wants me to go. But I feel as though I can't stand being away from the Father much longer..... *(laughs)* From You too. You see, You're being silly. You're not listening to me. You're just trying to be wise..... Of course I can't stand being away from You...... Dying is living – it is almost a contradiction..... I don't know. Why did He put the yearning in my soul?..... Butchie, You know something that You're not telling me..... First You want to tell me too much, and then when I want to know something, you stop telling me anything..... *(laughs)* Well, I don't want to know anyhow, so keep it there..... Yep, I'm sure that I don't want to know. So now You can start some other way to tease me.....

Yes, I do have that yearning so bad sometimes. I just want to cry and I feel so lonesome. I want to go to Him. I almost feel like begging, and I don't want to beg because I don't want Him to feel bad..... I know that there is so much more that I must learn and leave to His children, His people, my people..... I know that He has so much for me to do..... I remember that promise well, but I'm afraid to use it. I'd rather have Him do it..... No, the yearning is there and it grows..... Sometimes I wake up at night, Butchie, and I can't stand being without Him..... I know, but there's still a separation and this dopey body is the separation. I've got to shake it and get rid of it..... Only through death, I guess. Only through death I live. *(laughs)* That would make a good tape..... When I have time. I don't have time for anything, not the things that really count..... Yeah, that counts..... Sometimes I do resent being so busy, and yet I know that that's my vocation. I want so much for everyone to know His secrets, and I just don't have the time.....

No. I can't do that. The Father could. Talk to Him, Butchie..... You are full of delight in my refusing. Look at Your face..... Well, get a mirror and look at Your own face..... You just delight in my sticking with the Father. You're not kidding me..... I do love You so much, Butchie, and I love the Father..... I understand that. I had sorrow in my heart today when I was making that tape – to think that the Holy Spirit came in splendor and we rejected Him. That's just what Capi wanted us to do and we gave in. I feel bad. I feel as though the Father will withdraw His Spirit..... No, I don't mean that, Butchie. You do give me a hard time.....

Him, Father. He gives me a hard time all the time. He keeps telling me, and I'm going to squeal on Him, "Tell the Father that you want to come"..... Father, You're God. You know what I said..... For sure I do, Father. I love Him so much. Some times it's hard to refuse Him..... Not really. He just says that, because He knows that I want to do what my Father says, just like He does what the Father says. He's just teasing me. He likes to play games, Father.....

He said that if I really wanted to have quiet times I would have them..... You teach me so much in my quiet moments, Father, and I'm getting less peace than ever..... And if in the little quiet times, You can teach me so much, imagine if I had more quiet times, my Father.....

I reached for the star today and it was a little bit closer..... I think that I understand, my Father. I could stretch my fingers. *(laughs)* Or give me longer fingers. You're God. I would get there faster..... No. Whatever You wish..... Just at times I feel as though my heart's going to break if I stay here longer.....

You remind me of the baby. When she woke up this morning she said "Mama" and looked to the right and to the left. It's like when I wake up at night, I want to know You're there. And if I'm with You all of the time, I'll know that You're there. I just want to hear Your voice, Father.....

It seems the longer I stay here the more worries I get, Father. Look, I'm worrying about the priests, and about everybody now. I'm worrying about Muriel's kids and I'm worrying about this one who is calling me. I don't want to be tied down with worries. I want to pray for them and get back to You, my Father.....

See, we're bogged down with everything. I want them to be set free like I want to be set free just to love You, to seek You..... I sense a new plateau, this yearning, this craving, this wanting to be set free.... **A balloon. Let a rope go, one at a time, and then it's free.** Then cut the ropes. Then set me free, Father..... What rope is that, Father?..... My ministry? I don't know if I like that, Father. If that's the only thing that's holding me back. I don't know if I like it..... I don't mean to be serious..... You better explain that to me, Father..... **Through my ministry I'm bringing the word of the Father and revealing the Father to His people, and if You set me free they're going to lose the word.....** Then what You're really saying, Father, is that it's not time right now..... **You still have more work for me to do. You have freed me from all the ties of family. I can finally walk away from it knowing that they'll be all right..... The only thing that's keeping me tied down is the ministry.** That's because You want this for me, right?..... But when will You ever set me free?..... When will that be, my Father?..... **Your words will go on and on forever and there will be more and more people crying out for Your word.....**

I don't want to be a hundred years old. That's a long time. I'm not complaining. Do You think I'm complaining?..... **When I leave them enough food to make them crave the kingdom.** How?..... **In**

my ministry. The tapes. Videotapes. Then Your word will go on forever and ever. Then You'll cut me free, and they'll still have the word. So then You mean when I get enough stuff out about the Father and Butchie and the Spirit and the kingdom, between the tapes and the videos and the talks, when there's enough to feed Your sheep, You'll set me free, and I'll come like a balloon right back to the Father?..... Then we better hurry up and get all our stuff out..... **The audio and video tapes will go on forever** ..... That sounds cool.

The only thing that sounds really cool is that there's no other shackle that ties me down. And that's what You want from me. And it's good because I'm detached then. Right, Father?..... That makes me feel good..... Well, not that good, for sure. I'd rather be free. And if it was up to Butchie, He'd let me come now. See, Butchie, He's giving You the eye. You'd better watch it.....

I understand now. It's good to know that there is only one tie and it's for a good purpose, that people may know You, Father..... **I must reveal the kingdom to them, and the Father's love, the love of the Son. I must truly show them what the Spirit has meant in their life, and the purpose of the Spirit being renewed within their souls.....** Then the more I teach You, and the more tapes I get out, the faster I can reach that time when there will be no more ties holding me down?..... You promise, my Father?..... I know that You won't lie. You can't lie. You're God. I believe You, for sure..... Well, it makes me feel better. Not completely better, but real better.....

Butchie, You look so funny. Do You know what He's doing behind Your back, Father? He's showing me an axe, like He's going to chop it *(the tie holding down the balloon). (laughs)* It looks like He took a funny pill, Father..... Of course I love Him. I love Him and all His anxiousness for me to come. And I even love Your clowning, Butchie..... *(laughs)* Like we were kids again, huh?..... You can't say that, Father, You're God..... Did You hear what He said, Butchie? "God forbid." You can't say "God forbid." You're God.

You wouldn't want us to be kids again?..... *(laughs)* **It's better**

not having to watch us. Father, You're funny too. That's where Butchie gets His funniness, from You, my Father..... I'm very content that You told me. I know that there is a purpose and I'll do the best I can, my Father, and I know that You're going to help me. And I need the Holy Spirit. Don't withdraw Him from me, my Father. I certainly don't deserve Him, but I can't function without Him. And I love You, Holy Spirit. I need You so much..... I feel so bad about the Renewal. I'll make it up to You anyway I can, Holy Spirit, by listening to You and getting Your light and receiving Your light for the talks so that people will love them..... **You've sent Your Spirit upon me, and He'll pierce the depths of my soul. I will speak the wisdom of my God. I will reveal to God's people His kingdom. I will quiver in the sight of rejection, but I will grow strong.** Thank You, Father.

INTERVIEW

I'm happy with what the Father told you.

Right..... I have no attachments at all, except I'm tied down with my ministry and that's where He wants me to be tied down. He said I'm just like one of these big balloons that go up into the air with people in them. And He says I'm free on all sides but one, and that is the ministry, because He still wants to keep me linked with the ministry, to preach His word. And when I have enough talks out on my tapes and my videotapes, enough material to go on and on, when He thinks it's enough, He'll cut me free, and I'll go to Him.

But He better hurry up. You know what Butchie did? He was clowning around and He had an axe and He was touching the blade of the axe and He was looking at the rope tying the balloon. He made believe that He was going to chop it, until my Father gave Him the eye. And I said, Butchie, it 's just like we were kids again – always in trouble. And the Father said, "God forbid." And I said, "How can You say 'God forbid,' You're God." He said. "I had enough to watch when you were kids."

Butchie is so clowny. But it's good to know I'm not attached. He kept being lovey and trying to kiss me and to hold me and I wanted to talk business. He's so silly. But that's good to know *(when she will go to the kingdom)*. When my ministry, the Father's words, are out enough, and He knows they'll go on, that means the work will go on when I'm not here. It will go on and on. I won't be here, but the Father says that my words will be here and I can look down and see what's taking place. He's keeping me for my ministry, until He thinks there is enough stuff.

The first time He ever used the word "video."

He did say "videos." How did you know? I forgot. You listen to everything. Nothing's sacred around here.

The Father spoke about withdrawing the Spirit?

Yeah, He talked about that when I was doing a tape. I was worried about it. Not that He's going to withdraw the Spirit from the Church. Never. Not that He will withdraw the Spirit from a person who really craves the Spirit. But from these prayer meetings. He will stifle the gifts. He can do that if He wants. Because nothing is taking place, you know. Everything He gave us that was good, the devil twisted. We've become hypocrites. We're not changing. In the tape the Father said, "If it only took eleven apostles, because Judas was the outcast, to change the world, why can't we change the world with all these prayer groups going on?" He said, "Eileen, it's not doing what it was meant to do. Capi has won." Even the leaders haven't changed their lives. They're so successful trying to be leaders.

The Father spoke to you about not taking phone calls?

Capi is frustrating me by phone calls. I go crazy when that phone rings. And my kids are not trained, no matter how much I tell them. They called me out of the cellar to talk to M. I said, I just got through telling you. "Well, I didn't know her voice." Don't call me whether it's her voice or anybody's voice, I'm not here. I said, the only one you call me for is Father. Not anyone else. Not even Father X. because it's the same stuff. I no sooner tell them that and they call me. *(The phone calls prevent Eileen from doing her house work. Sometimes she is called from the cellar where she is washing clothes. Her children, like Eileen, are very obliging and don't want to disappoint a caller.)*

The Father spoke of Capi . . .

Capi. Oh, yes. He said, "Eileen, remember I told you that well meaning people would attack the Church? You're being attacked by well meaning people. M. is a well meaning person, and she sought your help. But after you hung up, you thought about her and your peace was disturbed." He said, "While you're thinking of that, you're not getting silence so I can work in you." So it's Capi attacking me through well meaning people. Good people. He's not going to throw some moron or some hobo at me.

So what does the Father want you to do?

Cut free from the good people. Pray for them. Don't take the phone.

GETTING TO THE VALLEY

January 29, 1984

Oh Butchie, I just marvel at the way You come running to me, as though I'm the only person in the whole world that counts, and I know You love us all..... *(laughs)* That's nice to hear. **It's just our valley. Nobody else counts in this valley..... You're waiting for me to come.....** Oh, it makes me feel important, it makes me feel loved, it makes me yearn to be here.....

You seem to be calling me more and more to the valley, as You did last night when I went to bed..... I think I have peace. Maybe not all the time, but within the depths of my soul I feel I have peace, right? But I know at my services sometimes I'm filled with anxiety and frustration..... I know, but I just can't help letting them become part of me. I'm in the world, Butchie, I'm not out of the world. And they're part of my life.....

For sure, I do. Good trick if you can do it..... **I'm listening. It's very important that you be drawn into this silence and solitude at this very hour. There is much to be accomplished in the valley of love and silence. There are many revelations to be revealed.....**

Of course I want to come to my Father..... Then we have to get this work done, and the faster we get the work done, the quicker I can come? That's a promise?..... **But I can't do it outside the valley.....** For sure I need silence, Butchie. You make me want to search for it *[silence]* more, if this is going to get me to the Father forever..... Then I must retreat, and do the Father's work fast, and accomplish all He wants me to accomplish. Then He'll take me, right?.....

Tell me about them, all the great things that You have in store for me..... Will they understand the revelations, Butchie? I don't know if they're ready for them..... In my talk? *(laughs)* ..... They were? Were You watching them?..... **They were eating it up** *(laughs)*..... The Bishop..... For sure. *(laughs)* A slip of the tongue and they enjoyed it? They were fascinated? The Father didn't mind?

You're delighted? Good..... *(laughs)*..... But I will. I'll really try to accomplish His work, as much as He wants me to accomplish, with the help of the Spirit. And then You promise I can come?..... **All the Father wants is for me to accomplish His work.....**

Thank You, Butchie, they're beautiful..... *(laughs)* I didn't do anything to merit that..... How do You know about my inner convictions?..... *(laughs)* More than anything in the world, I love You. You are so silly to keep asking..... I like to hear it too, You know..... There. That's real important to me, Butchie..... That means a lot to me, for sure..... That's how I feel, but we have to do my Father's work.....

(laughs) You sound like a conniver. Then there is a way of getting here faster, buckling down in silence and solitude and we'll accomplish it with the Holy Spirit and we'll get here faster, right..... I'm listening..... That's logical. **The Father has a set amount of work for me to do, and if I accomplish it, then He'll take me.....** But what about the Father's time, isn't He giving me a certain amount of time to accomplish it in?..... I will ask Him..... I know, Butchie..... *(laughs)* You're funny..... I didn't know the Son of God did that, I thought just people did that..... *(laughs)* Then what does He say?..... He calls You a conniver? He does? *(laughs)* The Father's stealing my words. You're funny. Butchie the conniver..... For sure..... No, what else does He say?..... *(laughs)* He says that? He says You're plotting to get me here sooner? You are funny..... **The Father loves the Son, the Son loves the Father, and they both love me.** Great..... Yes..... I'm all ears..... **In my silence and my solitude, my Father is going to lay forth His whole plan, and we're going to get it done as fast as we can, so I can get out of this world, and go to You, forever.....** *(laughs)* I wish You could do it in the blink of an eye.....

Nope, I get awful jealous when I hear everybody going to You, and I can't come..... For sure, I know that..... Well, whatever, they're coming to Heaven, and I can't come..... We'll do that, for sure. Everything. We won't leave a stone unturned. We'll do everything, everything the Father wants. Then He'll let me come. Right?.....

(laughs) We're agreeing on everything, Father. Not just one thing. Everything. Butchie says You have a whole plan for me, a function for me in my work and in my ministry, and that if I go into silence and solitude, the ministry and Your mission for me will be accomplished quickly because I'll not be distracted, and then I'll come to the kingdom quickly. Right?..... *(laughs)* You're funny too, Father.

Butchie said You called Him a conniver. What does He do?..... For sure?...... *(laughs)* And You know what He's thinking? Of course You know what He's thinking. **You look at Him and You say, He's planning to get Eileen up here fast.** Father, You're funny..... But I'll do what He says, if You agree. You agree?..... *(laughs)* Then we all agree. We're in agreement. And the Holy Spirit agrees.

Look at Him *[the Holy Spirit]*, Father. Isn't He wonderful?..... I know He's on my side. Last night He put the novena book in front of me three or four times, and I went right by it..... He just loves me to pray that novena to Him..... **He will give me the wisdom and the knowledge to function in the mission You have called me to.....** Butchie don't do that, the Father's talking to me. Be serious. Father, You've got a fresh kid here *(laughs)*.....

I don't understand why they talk about the Father and the Son as though You're just one, don't they know You're two persons?..... I love You all so very much. You're my whole life. Spirit, I could never function without You. I'm fully aware in my work, in my talks, that You're there with me, giving me the wisdom and the strength, and I love You so much that it blows my mind..... I know, Father, and it delights me that He's pleased. Words that I can't hear and yet, I know they're there. Love that I feel, I know it's there..... I understand, Father..... I know It is badly needed..... This year, Father?..... I get those words all fouled up, Father. I know it means to unite the churches, but I get them all fouled up. They're awful big for me to say, Father.....

The whole Church is going to try to be ecumenical, and they're going to destroy their own Catholicism. But not completely, Father. You said that the Church would never be destroyed..... **There'll be but a handful**..... I've heard that before, Father. Well, how will that do it?..... I know about losing our identity. Well, can't You send the Holy Spirit to them, and make them see they're wrong, Father?..... Well, make them pray with an open mind..... I know You can't force their will..... Well, what are we going to do about it?..... **Then, when they're ecumenical they have a very great danger of being too liberal.** Liberal in Church doctrine, in tradition?..... **Yes.**

Well, what can I do, Father? I'm nothing..... I'll do whatever He says, Father..... Won't I get clobbered?..... Oh, I don't mind being clobbered. I'm not saying I like it, now, so don't overdo it. I'm just saying I don't mind.....

I am? Well, it's because of You, my Father. I know how sound You are on doctrine and the tradition of the Church..... **But truly they must pray to the Spirit for enlightenment.** Can't He just zam them out?..... Oh dear..... **It's very hard to be ecumenical and not liberal, they're going to go together**..... Wait a minute now, please Father, I can't grasp all of this. **There's going to be a race for popularity.** The bishops? You're kidding..... That's awful..... That's terrible.

I won't waiver, Father, because the Holy Spirit will give me the grace not to waiver, Father, and I call upon Him all the time. I will be strong, my Father..... Oh, I depend upon Him to put the right words in my mouth, and I know this is what You have called me to..... Nope, I knew it was going to be a rough year, but I never imagined it was going to be this rough..... Who is that?..... **The new archbishop** ...... Right. Well, we'll pray and we'll sacrifice..... For sure, my Father..... Nope. Whatever You ask me to do, I will do, and I'll do it as fast as I can so we'll have that behind us and we can begin anew..... I'll pray for him too, Father..... I'm concerned..... Sure I'm concerned..... It's all right, Father, we'll do it. We'll do it together, because if You're with me, I'm strong..... **I have to be strong, and I have to be powerful, and I have to be loving, and I have to be firm.** That's asking a lot. That's a lot of ingredients in one person *(laughs)*.....

I won't *[ask what You want me to speak about]*, because I'll be all mixed up, like an egg beater. But I'll depend upon the Spirit to do it. Make me strong and make me firm and make me solid, but make me loving and outgoing, yet without wavering. See Spirit, You have a lot to do in me, and You better watch me real close.....

I just feel wonderful that You think I can do it, Father, and I know You'll give me the help, and it makes me feel important in Your love.....

Michael? Then I'm safe..... **He'll catch them in his hand.** *(laughs)*..... For sure I will..... With all my heart. *(laughs)* Even in spite of this mission, and I've got nothing to do with it, it's going to be a rough year.....

INTERVIEW

My Father says it's going to be a real rough year for the Church. I'm catching cold.

Wasn't Butchie rubbing your nose with some grass?

With a flower.

And the Father was talking to You?

He said it's going to be a rough year for the Church. He said it's all going to go in the direction of being ecumenical. And trying to be ecumenical we're going to be too free, and we're going to run into all kinds of trouble with doctrine and tradition.

He said it's already beginning. But He said some of those that are going to try so hard to be ecumenical will be stepping out of doctrine and tradition, and without realizing it, they're going to be liberals, and they're not going to come back because they want to be loved by all religions. That's bad, huh? That's really bad.

That's this year?

Yep, and He said, You are going to have to stand up there at your services. And I want more of My priests to come. He said that we have to to get back to being Roman Catholics. He said they *[ministers of other religions]* respected us more then. He said they're not respecting us anymore, like we're a past thing, Roman Catholic is a past thing. They're not respecting us anymore as they used to. So He said with our bending over to be too ecumenical, we're actually losing grace with them because they're not accepting us at all.

Well, the Father wants the union of all Christians, doesn't He?

Well, He used the word universal. He wants them all back into the Roman Catholic Church.

He wants them all back in the Roman Catholic Church?

Yes, because it's the true Church. And He used the word universal again. He said He didn't want us to be isolated from them. He wants to bring them into the Church. Roman Catholicism is the universal Church.

He wants the Church not to lose it's identity, and to bring them into our identity?

Yes. And He brought up about the Episcopalians, remember. And He said bringing them in *[as married priests]* has caused discord in the priesthood. There is a lot of discord in our Church over it, you know. Our priests resent it. He said, "Eileen, you've got to bring them back to the dignity of the priesthood."

Our priests resent that these men are married . . .

And have families, and they have homes, and they have the best of two worlds. They can go on the altar and everything. They have the best of two worlds, and the Father says our priests are resenting it, and this is going to be a year that we're going to lose even more priests than we have already. We've lost a lot, even in this diocese. And He said that I'm going to get clobbered.

What does He want you to do?

He wants me to talk about the Roman Catholic Church, and bring people into a deep love of the Church. Let them know what I stand for. He said, "Don't waiver, don't back down at all." But He said, "You're going to have many whiplashes, even in your own ministry." And when He said that, someone came to my mind.

They want you to be more ecumenical?

Yes, they think my ministry is too Roman Catholic. And He said I'd get a lot of suffering and heartbreak from my own, those that I love the most. But that's OK, because He'll be with me, and the Holy Spirit will be with me..... As long as I know what my Father wants, I'm going to do it. I'm not seeking a popularity contest. I tell the people that in my talks.

So He wants you in your talks to stand firm on doctrine and the tradition of the Church. And He wants more priests to come. And Butchie is conniving to get you into Heaven faster.

He said He has a plan. Be silent, and draw into solitude, and you'll hear the Father's word, then go out and do it fast. But if you have silence and solitude, you'll grab everything the Father has to say, you're not going to be distracted by people and telephones, and then we'll get this work the Father wants you to do done fast. He said, He didn't give you a time limit, He just wants so much accomplished.

In other words, when you accomplish it . . .

Then I can go. That's a good plan for sure.

So the Father called Him a conniver?

Yes, He said He was a conniver. He used the word "conniver." He said, "Eileen, I see Him quiet and He's thinking all the time and I know what He's thinking, but I ask Him. And He says: 'Nothing, Father.' The Father said, 'I know what You're doing, You're plotting to get Eileen up here faster.' My Father said He's been in a lot of deep thought lately. And I said, 'Gee, Father, I wish people would know You as the Father – and the Son and Holy Spirit. I wish they'd know Them. They know God, but they don't know them in their individual *[distinct]* persons.'" They're missing so much. The grace is there, but they're not accepting the grace. And the grace is there for the bishops to fight off being liberal.

The Father spoke about our becoming liberal?

Yes. Some say let's get on the same altar. Our churches are the same. They're not the same. Our doctrine and teachings are different, and our tradition is different. And we bend too far. The Father said man is causing discord in the Church.

How?

We're trying to cater to others, in the meantime, we're not doing what is right. Roman Catholics know what they're supposed to do, and they're not doing it.

You said, how can the Church be destroyed, it's supposed to last forever.

He said there'll be but a handful left. Because they're all trying to find a way out of confession, they're all trying to find an excuse for not going to Mass. "Hey, it's man-made. Who told you to go to Mass?" They're all trying to find excuses. And this is like the Protestants, they have communion once a month. And this is what's happening in our Church.

What was the slip of the tongue? Something about revelations?

Oh, I was saying in one of my talks that you could lie in the grass and the grass doesn't die, it snaps right up. People were looking and Butchie said, "Did you see them, Eileen, their mouths were open. They were thrilled at what you were saying."

I think I mentioned how I saw the snowbirds and sparrows *[feeding]* and big old blackbirds came and started taking all the bread. I threw rocks at them and said, "Get away from there." And my Father said, "Why are you doing that?" I said, "Father, they're eating all the bread." He said, "Eileen, don't you know they can't help what they're doing, even the birds have been touched by original sin."

In the kingdom, I said, all the birds live in harmony, and peace is in the air. Butchie was in front of me and He said, "Look, their mouths and their eyes are as big as saucers." They were thrilled that there is no fighting in the kingdom.

I said, "There is no eating of animals, either. You don't need to kill to eat. Everything is beautiful, and there's plenty. And the Father is there and He'll eat, because, as Scripture says, the Father has a hand, and He has a mouth, and He can put something in

His mouth." And Butchie said, "See how they eat up these things you're giving them. They want to know about the kingdom."

Does He want you to put out tapes?

He wants me to put out tapes. He wants me, every once in awhile, as the Spirit leads me, to tell them about the kingdom. I never plan to tell them anything. I can't say I plan anything. The Spirit leads me Himself. But they're hungry. They want to know about the love of God, and they want to get over this fear of death and to expect a great kingdom. They're afraid of the unknown, so you've got to make it known to them.

What was that about the Bishop?

Oh, I know. He said, You have a wonderful Bishop, he's kind and he's gentle and he's loving to those of all faiths. But he's a solid Roman Catholic Bishop. He's solid in doctrine and tradition. He's truly a Roman Catholic Bishop."

And Bishop Marshall?

He said he's a fine bishop. One of the finest, He said that to-night.

And He said Michael was going to help you in your work?

Yes, and He said he would catch the arrows of the devil. The devil tries to pierce you even through those you love. Michael will catch the arrows and I won't be hurt. *(laughs)* Good old Michael, I need him for sure.

Did the Spirit show Himself to you today?

Yes, as a silhouette. He really loves me, and I love Him, for sure. Last night, I went by the bureau, and my Holy Spirit novena was there. I looked at it and I heard a voice, "Eileen, open the book. Speak to Me." And I said, "Oh, later, I'm not in the mood now."

You walked by the book in your room, and He was there?

The Holy Spirit's voice. And I said, "Oh, I'm not in the mood." And I went by again, and He said, "Eileen, pick up the book." So I picked it up, and I read the consecration, and I read the prayers for the gifts and the fruits of the Holy Spirit, and the prayers to the Spirit. And I felt such a joy, and then when I went to lie down, there was Butchie. The Holy Spirit and then Butchie were preparing me for a peaceful night. I sat on the bed and I read the prayers and I could feel the joy of the Spirit. There's such a feeling in that book. I did it just to please Him. "Oh Eileen, pick up the book. Speak to me." I did, and then I was filled with joy.

[The book in question is a small booklet, Novena to the Holy Spirit *published by the Holy Ghost Fathers, 1141 Amherst Avenue, Wheaton, MD 20902.]*

TUNED IN TO THE FATHER'S VOICE

February 5, 1984

I was just thinking, Butchie..... I was watching Father break the Host, and I was wondering why You let us break up Your body so much, and the Father said, "It's not the hands of my priests that break the body, Eileen, it's the sins of the world." And that made me stop to think, Butchie.

I become oblivious to everything except You when I receive You. Butchie, why can't I be this way all my life?..... How can I do that?..... But I have to function in my vocation, that's what I'm supposed to do.....

(laughs) Of course I've heard of robots. Everyone has..... **I would be like a robot, functioning with perfection in my work, but be oblivious to everything around me except the sound of the master.** *(laughs)* That sounds pretty neat, if I could do it. I'd be doing my housework and my dishes and my wash, and not hear what's around me except my Father's word..... **Because a robot is subject to just one.** That sounds great..... No, I don't know how I can do it, but I'm certainly going to try. It sounds like a neat trick.....

Every moment of the day should be a communion. Then I should be so united with You, Butchie, that nothing else should get to me except the Father's voice. Just like a robot. Now I know. But how can I do this with all the distractions..... **I can do it by accepting the grace. Every moment should be a communion.** Every moment. I should be in communion with You every moment.....

Butchie, don't do that. I'm trying to think of what You said and that tickles my face. You always do this when You give me a thought. Then You try to distract me..... What else are You trying to do? I'm trying to grasp this. You know my mind isn't so great..... Every moment I should be in communion with You, Butchie, right? And the only thing that should disrupt this, it would be a disruption of love, would be my Father's voice, whom I'm tuned into, and who gives me direction. I shouldn't listen to anything around me, just function to the best of my ability in my vocation. That's what I'm keyed for or tuned into, right?..... It sounds pretty easy, but I don't know if I can do it.....

Butchie, knock it off. Do You want to teach me or do You want to fool around?..... *(laughs)* **Both.** I can't do both, I'm not that bright. So teach me first..... All right, I'm listening..... I learned that one. I hope I can do it. I need Your help and the Father's help and the Spirit's. Then I can actually become oblivious to everything around me like when You come into my heart in communion..... **It's up to me.....** I want to learn something else. Butchie, be serious and talk to me, I want to learn something else. This is serious stuff, You know, and I've got to know what it's about.....

Oh Butchie, I know they must have been in communion with You all the time, but I'm not up to them, I'm always doing something wrong. You have to work with me where I am..... Then it is possible..... **Being in the world and not of the world..... Consider myself a robot. I'm designed to do my work at home with perfection and love. But I'm not designed to answer the phone, or to talk to these other people, and the only voice I'm tuned into is the Father's voice and His teachings.....**

(laughs) I hope I've got it straight. I want to learn something else, Butchie. Talk to me. Teach me..... Teach me right. I'll tell the Father..... *(laughs)* One track mind..... *(laughs)*..... Sounds beautiful, but I want You to teach me something else, tell me something else.

This way I can be oblivious to everything around me like in the Eucharist, right? That's what I want to do, Butchie. Then we'll have all the time in the world for each other. See? Do You buy that?..... How could I put that across? *(laughs)* They wouldn't understand me. I don't think they understand me now..... **Who care?** I care. The Father cares and You care..... I worry a lot about it..... Maybe I shouldn't, but I figure if the Father sends them to me, then I have to feed them, right? And I have to listen to the Spirit, and make sure I know exactly what He's saying, and give it out just like He wants.....

I hope so. I hope so..... That's funny, I said that to Bee today. I told her she makes loving God too difficult, and it's very easy to love Him. She complicates things. Just like You're trying to complicate things. I'm trying to learn, and You're trying to mix me up..... *(laughs)*..... There You go on Your own track again..... Butchie, I love You so much, but I really want to learn so I can give it out. Don't You want me to give all this stuff out?..... *(laughs)* You told me that You wanted me to give everything I could to the people as fast as I could so I'd accomplish the Father's will. So that's what I'm trying to do. OK..... Right now, down to business. **We're going to strive for this union and let everything be outside of us, and nothing will get through except the Father's word, because I can't function without His word. When He tells me to function, I will function. I won't let man drive me, just the Father**..... I like that more and more. Well, we're in agreement

Butchie, I love You so much. There's nothing in the world I like more than to spend all this time with You, but I have to learn if I want to come here fast, and I have to know what to teach God's people..... You gave me the recipe how to get here fast, and now You want to switch and You're stopping me..... *(laughs)*..... Nope..... I'm trying to follow all the ingredients *[of Your plan]* so I'll get here.....

You have? Tell me about it..... How early?..... **Around four**. That means I'd have to go to bed early. I don't get very much sleep as it is, Butchie..... Now this is good what You're saying, and I'm listening, Butchie..... **Get up early, an hour before them, sometimes two, if they go to bed later. And that's the hour I'll tape. Let the dogs out and let them run.** That's a good idea. See, Butchie? I knew You'd come up with something..... *(laughs)* Tell me some more. That's a good one. That's one good hour. Think of something else. That's beautiful.....

Of course I'll do it, I'd love to do it. When everything's quiet. That's beautiful..... I don't know exactly what time..... **At one.** That's right they do. There is an outlet there..... That would give me an hour. Then I'll take the nap..... *(laughs)* Yes, go to the valley. You're always a step ahead of me. That's beautiful.....

(laughs) Look, Father, Butchie's telling me all the things I should be doing, and He found two hours that I can tape, Father, and do your work. *(laughs)* Really..... Now how could You think that?..... **You know what He's thinking. That's what He was plotting.....** Yes, my Father. I know that He wants me to come fast, but He's also aware of the work You have planned for me, my Father...... I'm just delighted. I want to do everything You want me to do.

I love You so much, my Father. All I want to do is to please You and to do Your work..... At any cost, Father. Well, yes, I do worry about it. It bothers me that I can't seem to draw as many people as these jazz singers, and theirs is just for nutty stuff, and mine is for You, Father. You should have the biggest audience in the whole world..... But I want it to be for good and right reasons, Father. For You, Father, and for Your love. I want them to know You as I know You. I don't want them to come and just look at me, or see a show, or snatch a miracle. I want them to come because they hunger for You, Father.....

Thank You, Father. that pleases me so much..... I know it will be difficult, but we'll stand by our guns, Father..... Nope, I won't waver, no matter what..... I do feel sorry for them, because they're confused and it's Capi that's confusing them He's really a bad guy, Father..... No..... I know. They're so fouled up..... **A tape on this.....** I don't have the wisdom to cut through this stuff..... **The Spirit has the wisdom.....**

How could I do such a tape, Father, without offending..... **The Spirit never offends.....** I know. I have to be careful, Father..... I understand, Father..... I don't mean to look glum. I'm just trying to figure out what's going to take place, and I know I shouldn't try to figure it out, because the Holy Spirit will take care of me..... I don't forget for a moment that I'm His bride. Who can have so many husbands and be legit, Father?

(laughs) You look so beautiful when You smile..... Nope. You look beautiful when You don't smile. You look beautiful all the time, but I love to see You smile..... O Butchie! See how He is, Father?..... *(laughs)* Butchie, cut it out..... See? See? He says when You smile I say You're beautiful, when He smiles, I say He's fooling around..... *[The Father asks if she loves His Son]* Of course I do *(laughs)*.....

Yes, He told me about it..... I'm delighted. I never could have thought of that in a million years..... I think it's beautiful..... *(laughs)* Yes, leave it to Him..... See, Butchie, the Holy Spirit works with You, too, so don't give Yourself all the credit..... *(laughs)* Look at the way He's pulsating..... You're the Son of God, so You have to stay humble. So knock it off..... Isn't He silly, Father..... *(laughs)* I like the way You say that..... We'll try it.....

I know You do, Father, and I love You too. So very much..... Yes, I understand..... I know You will, Father..... **Hope** *(laughs)* That would be a funny name, but if You wanted it, You should have inspired my Mother..... *(laughs)* That would have been cute. I like that name, Hope..... **Hope for the world.** I don't know if I'd like the last part, but I would like Hope. It's really pretty, especially coming from You, my Father..... Is that what You think?..... That thrills me to death. You know just the right things to say to me, Father.....

I guess we do know what we're about..... I guess that's all that's important..... That sounds beautiful, but You never told me that before..... Every time You hold me so close, I'll be thinking of that. **There is hope. Hope for the world.** It's almost like a melody, Father. It makes this moment more precious, peaceful, and joyful.

INTERVIEW

My Father teaches me when I'm home and I'm resting on my bed. He takes me to my valley. Communion is a love-time for me and Butchie. A lot of times we stay in the brook and play. A lot of times we just walk and we talk and we love and we visit different plateaus to see what's going on there.

Do you visit people when you go to different plateaus?

No, they can't see me, but I can see them.

Can you see what's going on at the different plateaus?

Yes, I can see what's going on. I can see them, but they can't see me. And the only reason my Father lets me see them is because *[otherwise]* I couldn't understand their spirit. They're going to have their glorified bodies later. But there is a different way you can see them with their spirit. It's different. They have on robes, but it's almost like a flowing robe, there's nothing underneath. But He allows me to see their faces.

I remember once I saw a beautiful lady. They all look about the same age, about thirty-three. And she had feet, and she had her hands like this holding water in some kind of a container. I saw her arms, and yet, I knew there was no body under that garment. Her feet were not on the ground. I saw her arms holding that container, and her beautiful and flowing hair. But there was enough breeze to show that there was nothing in that garment. I see that a lot.

I said to Butchie, How come she doesn't see me? And He said, Because she's in a different dimension. You're not in her world yet. And I said, How come I can see her? He said, because I'm allowing it. And she walked right by me without looking at me. And as the wind blew, I knew there was nothing in that garment.

Sometimes my Father and I just sit, and He holds me, and He talks about the world, and what He really intended for the world, and His saddest thing is the sin of the world. Sometimes He tells me they don't understand He's a loving Father, and that is sad. He says they talk about God like He's a fiction, and that saddens Him. He wants so much for the people to know Him, and they don't know Him.

That's what He said today. He said, "You know, Eileen, Your name should have been Hope. Because when I hold You in my arms, I feel there is hope for the world." Wasn't that beautiful? It gave me such a thrill. I think every time He holds me now I'll think of Hope.

Hope for the world. It's so beautiful, it's almost poetic. I said "Father, You never said that before." He said, "But I'm saying it now. Every time I hold You in my arms and I press you close to Me, I say, There's hope for the world."

Perhaps He means through your mission?

Probably.

So Butchie had an idea about how you could tape.

Yes, He did. He is so funny. He said to me, "The Father laughs, and you say, He's beautiful. I laugh, and you say, Stop fooling around." He said, "Father, there's no justice here, and this is Heaven!"

What did the Father say?

The Father laughed. "He said, Listen to my Son. 'There's no justice here.' " Then He said, "Did you learn your lesson well?" I said, "Yes, that was a real neat thing about the robot." He said, "Eileen, be like a robot. That robot is only subject to the authority of the one who built it." He said, "The Father created you. Block out everything. Do your work to the best of your ability. The oil for the robot is the grace that the Father gives you, that I won for you on the cross. But don't listen to any of the people in the world, they are going to confuse you. Robots can't listen, they're only tuned in to the master. You only be tuned in to the Father. So block out everything. This is the way you become oblivious to everything and in total communion with God. Get away from them all. Function to the best of your ability by grace, the oil that keeps the robot going, but the only one who can control the robot is the Father. And the only voice you're going to hear is the Father's voice. Block out everything, the telephone."

He said that's been done before?

Yes. This way I become oblivious to everything, I block out everybody, and I'm tuned in, listening to the Master.

Did He tell you who did that?

Butchie did it.

Butchie did it?

He did it. The only one He heard was the Father's voice. He wouldn't listen to men. They were saying He wasn't the Son of God, He wasn't this, He wasn't that. Even Peter tried to sway Him. The sons of Zebedee, the mother of the sons of Zebedee, they all tried to sway Him. But He only listened to His Father's word. To nothing else.

Doesn't He speak through people?

Yes, but He's not speaking through people to me right now. He's speaking directly to me. These people are confusing me.

They're saying something different from what He's saying to you?

Yes, Bee confuses me. She's a good lady and she really means well. She does all good things, but she makes loving the Father so difficult. I said to her this morning, Bee, you make loving God so difficult.

And did the Father or Butchie say that to you today?

The Father did. He said, "They all confuse you, Eileen. They're mixing you up, all those telephone calls." He mentioned Joan again, too, and He said, "They're confusing you."

Well, what does He want you to do?

See, if I'm a robot, I'm not going to listen to them.

You won't take the calls?

No, I won't take the calls at all. I'm only tuned in to the Father. He said be only tuned in to Him, to His voice. Then He said, "Which one has taught you something this week?" None of them have taught me anything. They pull me down. A team leader *[of the prayer group]* announced: "If Eileen were generous, she would give every talk during Lent." That means I'm not generous. So I felt really whacked out with that thought. I felt really, Wow, what a low blow. But it's not the Father's will.

What was Butchie's proposal about how to get time for taping?

Oh, early in the morning. Get up before the family is up. They're all in a deep sleep. They don't start stirring until the alarm goes off at six. So I can have two hours before that to tape. Let the dogs run,

He said, and they'll come back. Because otherwise they'll be whining to go out, especially in the summer. I love that time of the morning. That was a good idea. And the girls watch the soap box operas which go on at one, so they eat around twelve. So while they're eating, He said, I can tape. I can go down to the cellar in the back room, and I can tape. I can get another hour of taping, Butchie said. And then come upstairs while they're watching it and take my nap.

At two o'clock?

No, at one. He insists that I take my nap because that's a priority of the doctor. I loved that about the robot. There was another one He told me. It was important. Oh, that I should make a tape about the confusion in the Church. And I said, Butchie, that's a very difficult thing. And my Father said, Eileen, do you think anything is too difficult for the Spirit? And I said, but that is so touchy. And He said, it doesn't have to come out now, but I want you to make it now. And He said everything would be kosher according to doctrine, and not to worry about it.

The robot isn't for everybody, because some people have to listen and discern whether God is speaking through other people.

I know. This is Him talking to me. I can't say what He does with other people.

How about listening to me?

He wants me to listen to you, for sure.

Did He say that?

Yes, but you're not there all day. When I'm up on the podium, people say, Eileen, you're radiant. You look like you're talking to us, but you're not with us. It looks like you're in a different world, and you're listening to the Father. So I guess that's what Butchie means. Be in the world, but not of the world.

What did Father H. say?

Father H. always says the moment you walk up to that podium, it's almost like you're a different person. He said, "You talk so leisurely, so openly, so relaxedly, I just can't get over it." He said, "It's what every preacher wants, and can't acquire." But he also said, which makes me feel great, "You can tell it's the Spirit. He overshadows you and you're completely different up there. You're so nonchalant and peaceful." Most of the priests tell me that. "Eileen, you talk with such ease, such grace." It makes me feel good, but I know it's the Spirit. I know it's the Spirit for sure, because there are theologians there, there are doctors there. I know I'm not educated like they are, and yet, nothing bothers me. That doesn't even come to my mind. The Spirit's moving.

That's the way He wants you to be.

That's the way my Father wants me to be. I'm truly overshadowed by the Spirit.

What did the Father say when you said to Him, "You're just fooling around. You know everything. You know what He's thinking."

Oh, I know what it was. He said, "All day He's been plotting, and I said to Myself, Is He plotting to get Eileen up here faster?" I said, "Oh Father, come on, You can read His mind, you know He was thinking about the robot." The Father laughed and winked at the Son. They love each other.

What did the Son say?

You've never seen such love as between them. It's beautiful. It's the way they respond to each other. We look at God and Jesus as stuffed shirts, stiff necks. And they are so beautiful and so loving. So full of real life, not the garbage we have down here. Real life, where true happiness is.

They fool around with each other?

They laugh and they joke. Everything in Heaven is beautiful. They have everything they want. They have the joy, the laughter. Everything except what comes from sin, which is sadness and pain. That's excluded. Everything else. It's humorous, it's joyful, it's witty. Everything to make you happy is there. Or else it would be boring. Everything is beautiful. People can't understand this. They don't know this. The Father jokes with the Son, and the Son jokes with the Father. They never get angry with each other, because anger comes from sin. That would be a good tape, too. Anger and all our passions come from sin. So if you want to be with God, you erase them, and when you erase those things, then you're with God. But while we hang on to them, we're being tied down to earth by sin.

And that's what He meant, too, when He said don't linger with anything, don't be tied down?

That's right, don't linger. Like, Bee calls me up to talk this morning. Her conversation takes part of my mind away from God because after she hangs up what she said comes back to me. That's what the devil wants. The more you mingle with people, their thoughts get embedded in your brain, and your mind is so taken up during the day with what this one said and what that one said.

Even these boys at my house *[two boys thrown out of their home by their stepfather because of their behavior, taken in by Eileen]*, they're boggling my brain so I can't think straight. This is what Capi wants, because while they're boggling my brain, that part of me is not thinking of my Father. So now I don't even yell at them when they stay out late. One said to my son, "Your mother doesn't know I came in late, because she didn't say anything." I knew, but I'm placing it in the probation officer's hands. See? I call up the probation officer and I say, This is what they've done. Take care of it.

It reminds me of Sister A. All she talks about is the ministry she is in. All these people who call, you can't help but talk to them. Then after you hang up you think for about ten minutes or twenty minutes or an hour during the day, off and on, what this one said. And that's time taken away from the Father. But if I'm a robot, like Butchie says, only my Father can get through to me.

Would you still be talking with these people?

Nope, I shouldn't talk to them.

When you were thinking that more people should come, and they should come because of hunger for the Father, the Father said something to you and you said, "Thank You, Father, that pleases me so much."

Yes. He said everyone that comes to my service goes away hungering and thirsting for a deeper love of the Father. And I said, "Father that thrills me, You know." And He said, "Yes, Eileen."

IN LONELINESS MY JOY WILL SPRING FORTH

April 26, 1984

I know, but there's not too much I can do about it, Butchie . This is my rest here with You..... Maybe deep down I'm aware of it, but I'm not aware of it all the time..... Sometimes I think if I rest, I'll never get up again. And I get up so sick. At other times I don't want to rest.....

I know You love me..... Yes, I know how concerned You are about me..... No, I didn't understand that. You mean if I don't rest I won't last this year?..... Well that's good, I'll be with You..... **That's not the Father's will for me. I must do my work.** My ministry? You mean just by not resting, I could die?..... Nope. You're not frightening me, I'll be glad if I die. Then I can be here with You all the time. First You want me to come, and now You're telling me all the precautions to take. You better make up Your mind, McGee.....

I know, the Father has work for me to do, and I certainly want to do everything He wants me to do..... I didn't think you could die from lack of rest..... **Ordinarily not, but in my case yes.** Why?..... **I have low immunity.....** Rest will stop that?..... I don't mean to question You, I just wanted to know why rest is so important for me.

Not that I don't like it. I do love it, Butchie , but then I get up so sick..... If You say so..... I'm so glad You're back. I don't want You to preach to me today. I just want You to sit with me and walk with me. You've got the whole year to preach to me. You'll be all preached out..... I don't think I'm silly, I think I'm truthful, Butchie. I don't want you to be preached out, so don't preach today, preach tomorrow.....

(laughs) Thank you..... I love You too, Butchie . I missed you so much. I'm still shaking inside at the thought of You leaving ever again..... Well, it didn't seem like it bothered You that much. You only came back once or twice..... Nope, I don't doubt Your love. Not even for an instant, Butchie, I never have. I sometimes chirp off, but I don't mean it, and You're God, so You know I don't mean

it. Just getting even, I guess, or trying to.....

Were You really lonesome?..... How could You be? You could walk in the valley without me..... Do You really mean that? It's not the same here without me? And it's not the same when You walk by Yourself? That's how I felt. Everything is still so beautiful, never been touched, and yet, the beauty of Your presence was gone. It was like the luster was gone.....

There was peace, sure, and beauty, but nothing matters without You, Butchie . And You better not do it again..... Well, You can call it a threat. Do what You want. Tell the Father..... I just might do that. Do You think I'm afraid?..... *(laughs)* You know I'm not afraid. I love the Father.....

That's very nice. It seems all worth while when You hold me like that, but then it makes it worse when You're gone..... I know, but after awhile it hurts too much. Don't You think so?..... I'd rather not have a homecoming, I'd just rather have You here all the time, and not take off any more. It's like You divorce me every year. I thought there'd be no divorces in Heaven. You're starting a new fad, Butchie. You'd be surprised how quickly these things catch on, even in Heaven. It'll go from one plateau to the other, and You'll be the cause of it.....

Nope. I just don't want to talk about it any more. No new fads. That's it..... No, I don't think it's cute. I'm mad You know..... *(laughs)* I will put on a mad face, then what are You going to do?..... *(laughs)* Butchie, You're funny..... No more talking about that. We'll talk about the valley. It was so awful here without You..... *(laughs)* Did You really? Don't do that. Don't do that.....

(laughs) I wasn't talking to myself, I knew You were sneaking around some place, listening. You almost cracked up?....*(laughs)* I didn't feel like cracking up. I was really mad. I was trying to prove to myself I was getting along without You..... You're funny..... Really? Then why didn't You come forth?..... **Father said "No"**..... *(laughs)* Is that right?..... You did? He didn't tell me that. That proves the Father loves me, right?..... Were You really? I didn't feel You at

all..... I knew You'd be listening..... Well, after You come back, I'll walk away from You and see how You like it. Even steven..... I don't care if there's a true Lent, I'll make my own Lent. Then there'll be two. You do it the first time, and I'll do it the second time..... Well there won't be the resurrection until I do it the second time to You. See if You like it.....

(laughs) You are funny. I love You so much. I'm so glad You're home..... It didn't seem that way. I was so lost and so lonely. Like I died inside. Just going through the motions of living. Not really living, just pretending I was living. It was awful..... But I didn't feel like You were. It's easy for You to say. I couldn't even stimulate my faith, and that's pretty bad..... I know, but it's pretty hard to remember that in a time like that, Butchie .....

(laughs) I was really mad..... *(laughs)* You didn't like standing on Your head?..... I thought of it at the spur of the moment. Remember when I was a kid, what I used to do – stand You on Your head..... I got the idea when I stood You there..... He did laugh? Poor Father. What He has to put up with, with me..... *(laughs)* All I had to hear was Your laugh and I would have been better, but You wouldn't even let me hear that.....

Butchie , this is no time for kissing, this is a time for scolding. And I'm scolding You. Don't You ever do it again..... No, don't You ever do it again. I'll be mad. Real mad. Very mad..... Never mind. Twice as mad as that. Madder than madder than mad.....

(laughs) That's funny. Get off of that ground and stop acting so dummy..... I'll scare You, I'll bop You in the nose. Get up here..... That's better. I love You so much. I wish everyone could see how wonderful You are. How funny, and yet, how beautiful You are. How loving and full of fun You are..... Is that truth?..... No, I know You don't speak fibs. But it seems like everyone I know wants to know You, but You're not revealing Yourself. And yet, You say You reveal Yourself by grace as much as they want to accept You. So that means they truly don't want You to reveal Yourself, or it's just a habit.....

I think I understand. If they really wanted You to reveal Yourself to them, they'd be so good and practice virtue. But I'm not good, and I'm far from practicing virtue. Most of the time I'm squawking and complaining..... I know You love me, but don't I have to obey the rules too?..... *(laughs)* Oh no I'm not. How can I be an exception when You punish me so badly by hiding on me..... Aha! You're using my expression, "One track mind." I'll never forget it, so You better watch it.....

So to get back to the revealing subject, Butchie. People say, "Reveal Yourself to me, Lord." They mean it in words but they don't mean it by action or deed. So if I say, "Reveal Yourself to me," I must prove that I want You to reveal Yourself by my deeds? And what are my deeds?..... **Sacrifice, penance, prayer, but above all, loving and kindness and generosity, and then You'll reveal Yourself..... Because You know it's an act of truth and that they want to be true followers of Yours.**

Maybe they need a teaching on this, Butchie? I'll make one if You want me to, but You'll have to send the Spirit and give me the right words to say..... I'll do that..... I don't know where I'm going to get the silence, but I'll find a way..... I will, I promise.....

(laughs) Hi, Father, I'm promising Him that I'll make a tape..... "When Butchie Revealed Himself to Me"..... Father, You already know what I'm going to put in that tape, You're God. Did You forget You're God? And You ask me what I know? I don't know, but You know..... Yes, I'm loving Him..... I missed You both so terribly, my Father. The valley didn't seem the same. I didn't even want to come here any more..... Yes, I told Butchie there was beauty, but there was something missing, and that something was You and Butchie . The beauty was there, but the luster was gone. The fishes were there, but something was gone. And yet, in their beauty, I knew You were around, Father.....

(laughs) You're funny. Did You really?..... See, Butchie , the Father tells me everything. How do You like that?..... Really? Ever so many times?..... You didn't!..... I wish I had known that then, my

Father..... Does it really hurt You to hide on me..... **Yes.** Then why do You do it, huh?..... Oh yeah. Well, why don't You let me pick my way of growing once in awhile.....

I don't want to hurt You that way, Father. Can't I grow another way?..... No. Not for a minute, my Father. I just love You so much, and if it hurts You so bad to hide on me, I think You'd better not hide any more..... *(laughs)* Am I a fox? If I'm a fox, it's because You're my Father, and I take after You, my Father. You're the fox of foxes, and I want to be like You, so I'm a little fox, and You're a big fox..... Thank You.....

I really think You better not hurt Yourself so much, and You better stay with me all the time..... Well fox or not, You taught me what I know..... I know. I think I know a little bit how much You love me, and I make it ever so big in my mind..... I wish I could grasp it, but I can't grasp it all. I know You love me, but I know there's so much more, Father. I feel it in Your touch and in Your look.....

Of course I'm happy. You're here with me. I'm always happy when You're with me, Father. I'm so miserable when You're not here. It's like it's raining in my soul. But when You're here, the sun's shining, and I'm happy and I'm warm. When You take a powder, I'm wet and damp and so cold. All I do is shiver, and feel like I'm in darkness.

But now, I feel great. Do You feel great?..... We both feel great. We didn't ask You, Butchie , but we know You feel great too. He's always got to butt in..... You heard that? *(laughs)* I just told Father that You're always butting in. *(laughs)* Oh Father, You've got such a Son, but I love Him.....

Really? If You say so, Father. **There's going to be a good year ahead for me. My mission will be strong and will be powerful. The priests are starting to sit up and take notice, and see that the Father is working in me, and that I speak nothing but His love for His people.....** I think that's beautiful, Father.....

Butchie advised me that if I didn't rest, I wouldn't last a year.....

Well of course I believe Him, He's Your Son..... No, I said that when I rest, I get up feeling so sick, my Father. I know I need the rest, but I hate the sickness when I get up, so deathly ill..... I try so many times, Father, and I know I'm making an excuse, but there's always something. Always something.....

Of course I want to do Your work, Father. I love You, and I don't see why You keep asking me..... Yes, I do. For sure I do..... Yes, my Father, I really will try hard..... Yes, I understand that..... I wouldn't mind if I didn't last a year, but I do mind if I didn't do the work I'm supposed to do for You, Father. That bothers me for sure. Not lasting a year doesn't scare me a bit. I wouldn't care if I only lasted a day, my Father..... *(laughs)* We didn't ask You, Butchie ..... He's so cute. He listens all the time..... Look at Him, He's always acting cute, my Father..... Did He? Did He really miss me terribly?..... *(laughs)* You did? You had to pull Him by the shirt tail? What was He going to do?..... *(laughs)* Really? You're funny..... No..... You were having so much fun, and I was in agony..... Uh huh, so that's how You play the game, heh? You two were having a ball, and I was in agony.....

Of course it delights me now, Father, but it would have delighted me more if You'd have just let Him come, and didn't pull Him by His shirt tail. Let Him come.....

This year? If You say so..... **I must not let anyone drain me.** What do You mean by drain, my Father?..... **Call me day after day with the intention of praying or just chatting**..... .Yes, I do. I get a headache afterwards, when they're draining me..... **Try not to be so available on the telephone**..... *(coughing)* I will..... I know how much You and the Son love me..... I love You both so much. I tease You, Butchie, but You know how much I love You. And I love You, my Father. I almost felt like I was dying this time, and that makes me realize even more how much I love You both, and I want to give this love to Your people, my Father.....

What?..... I understand what You're saying. I could very well teach them the pain of loss of their God when they walk away from

Him by sin..... I know, my Father, I didn't sin. It was a terrible emptiness..... I very well could make them understand how we need Him to be happy..... And You, Butchie, how You're alive, and You're real, and You're moving, and You want to be so much a part of our lives..... I will do the best I can, my Father. You must send the Holy Spirit upon me. It's hard to function without Carsha. I can't spiritually function at all without Him..... You will? Thank You, Carsha. I depend upon You so much.....

I don't know if there is any more that I can see in You, Carsha, but I feel as though You're going to reveal more of Yourself..... Yes, Father. I know He has revealed more to me of Himself than to anyone else, but I still feel selfish, my Father, I know there's more He wants to reveal to me of His being the third Person. I know there's something deep He's trying to reveal to me, and He's going to..... Am I selfish for wanting this, Father?..... Is this really You *[putting this desire in my heart]*?..... Then I feel at peace, Carsha, and I do want to know You more as the third Person..... It's good for all of us to be together. Now my life is rich and full. I missed You all so terribly, I just can't seem to get over it.....

Oh my Father, why did it hurt so much this time? It hurt every time, but this time was the worst of all, my Father..... Sure..... **It's because my love has grown much deeper over the years that it is unbearable to be without the three of You.** That makes me feel good, but the pain was awful. **And the greater my love grows for You, the worse my suffering will be.** There's a touch of joy there. Should it be there, my Father?..... **Because in the isolation and loneliness, my joy will spring forth because I know it is the overwhelming love of my God that leaves me** *[feeling so]* **empty**. That's kind of deep, Father. So I need Carsha's light..... I have a deeper love for You, Carsha, since Lent, a deeper love for You, and I thank my Father. You're so important to me. I love You.

It's so good to be together again. Butchie, to have You so near. And my Father, to be in Your arms. And feel the warmth of Carsha's love and light. I don't want to be separated again, Father..... It was just like the stars never shone. It was like I was in darkness, but now I'm in light. Your faces radiate love. I want You to hang on to me and never let me go.

QUEEN FOR A DAY

May 6, 1984

I'm very happy to be here. I wish I could come more often..... Oh, sure I'm tired..... You're with me all the time, and You know what I have to do. Don't You think I should be tired?..... It's not a tired tiredness, but a joyful tiredness, Butchie. I am fulfilling my vocation, and it's my vocation to keep running and to do all these things.....

(laughs) That's my vocation too. And I love through my work. *(laughs)* You are funny. I'm talking serious and You want to love. I'm talking serious, Butchie. I'll tell the Father. You are always getting me off the track.....

I love You too, Butchie. I would certainly like to be here all the time. I realize more and more that I want to be here all the time. Not too much has meaning for me any more..... Is He really putting that desire in my heart?..... Thank You..... I understand, it's His work.....

Yep, I understand that. Sometimes I get down over it. I want more people, and more people don't seem to be coming. Oh, there might be a handful more, Butchie. Why can't I fill that church?..... Why is it so difficult for them to know You and to love You?.....

I understand that, Butchie. I know the Father has dealt with me in a different way, and I know You have too, Butchie..... But sometimes they seem so cold. I wish I could get through to them. They are as hard as nails, and distracted by everything. And I get down about it..... Instead of rejoicing with You, they're tied down, and they are tying me down. And I want to be set free.

Butchie, don't do that. I'm talking and I'm serious now. I'm real serious, You know. I'll tell the Father. Butchie, what can I do?..... I love You. I mean besides that. C'mon, what can I do?..... What's the matter, don't You think I love You enough?..... *(laughs)* You're funny..... I mean besides loving You..... **Just loving. That will take care of everything**..... For sure?..... All right, I'll concentrate just on loving You. I'm not going to worry about the church..... Then what are You going to do if it's not filled?..... I'll stand on Your word.....

(laughs) You are funny. **Just keep loving You and falling deeper in love with You. It's going to reflect to the people and more and more will come.** It's that easy?..... Nope, I didn't expect to get the answer out of a book. Just love You and that will draw them to me, and they'll hear the word of the Father through the light of the Spirit, right?.....

I don't know..... **My love of my Father, that's what's drawing them.** I'm amazed, not stunned, but amazed, that my love for the Father should draw them, when He's their Dad too..... **He's revealed Himself to me.** But what about: Nobody gets to the Father except through You? You said it Yourself..... **They see the love that I hold for You.....** Well, that's beautiful, Butchie. It sounds so simple..... I told them that by going to the Eucharist and by spending more time with You they'd fall deeper in love with You.....

Butchie, I spend a lot of time with You..... *(laughs)* Silly!..... That's a remedy all right..... What could possibly happen..... **Lots of stuff.** Like what, Butchie?..... But why are they leaving, Butchie? ..... Well, what about the devil? I don't like to talk about him in this valley..... **He's got till October.** What's going to go on until October?..... **Priests are going to leave between now and then, and nuns.....** Do You feel sad about it, Butchie ? Your face looks sad..... No, I feel sad, because You look sad..... Then what can we do about it?..... I've been doing that, Butchie. **Just love You for all those who do not love You.....** And how can that change things, Butchie?..... **It keeps the chastisement of the Father away.** Just from my loving You?..... I didn't mean "just." Saying it is a habit of mine, Butchie..... Well, I see You are upset because You're picking on me..... I know You don't.....

Loving You is the most important thing in my life. Praising You and the Father is the next most important thing..... Because in loving I'm pleasing, that's why I put it first..... How can I make my talks stronger by loving You? **That will make my talks stronger and**

more powerful. By loving You, spending more time with You.....

Don't say that, You make me feel real sad..... I don't know. Maybe five *[phone calls]*, maybe ten before twelve o'clock. Not so many between twelve and two, but some after supper. **All that time should be spent in loving You.....** I know, Butchie, Father said the same thing. It could be Capi, and You're confirming that it is..... It's so hard for me, Butchie, to let go. I need Your help real bad in this..... It'd be easier not to take the calls, but once they get me, I'm so afraid I'm going to hurt them..... Yes, I notice that..... Butchie, You've made it so important to me. I didn't realize talking to them took time away from loving You. I'm truly sorry, Butchie. I never looked at it that way.....

Repeat, what?..... **"Eileen, the more time You spend in loving Me, and the less time You spend in talking to your people, the more your love will grow, and it makes Me more the center of your life. It is not always a good angel that is sending these people to you. They are distracting you from My love."**

I don't want to be distracted from Your love, Butchie. And if talking to these people distracts me, then I won't talk to them anymore..... And I love You so, all my attention should be given to You, not to these people...... **Love them only by prayer.** Will they still be my friends, Butchie ?..... **It will hurt and they will kick and storm for a while. But then they will realize this isn't your mission. My first mission is loving You, dedicating my whole life to You and to attention to You, and then my words from the podium will be strong when I preach the Father, because I have the backing of Your love.....** You're real serious, You know. I love You. But I don't like You to be so serious with me..... Yes, I think loving You is serious business.....

Nope, I'm not mad. I love You, I'm not mad. I'm just listening, Butchie. Why do You ask me if I'm mad, You're supposed to know me, You're supposed to know everything..... You can't be jealous, because You're God..... *(laughs)* You are funny. You know that?..... *(laughs)* You do? *(laughs)*..... You are delighted? I'm glad someone is delighted. You're funny. As long as you are happy, Butchie..... Nope. I think You taught me a lot. My first mission is to love You and to be with You. And then in this love, in being with You, and always in Your presence, I can speak powerfully to my Father's children as a body, as a group, but not on an individual basis. And Your love will carry me through this. **It's very important that I learn this between now and the month of October. This is going to be a key to victory.** Over Capi?..... **(laughs)** You're funny. Well, if You say so, I agree with You..... Can't You tell me more about it?..... **You will, probably, You will tell me more about it.**

See, You were listening all the time, Father..... So much must happen between now and October? Father, You can make everything good happen, because You're God..... What does that mean?..... You are giving us the choice, that's what it means, Father? **You're not going to give us Heaven on a silver platter**..... I don't hold anything against You, Father, You know the secrets of my heart. I know You are just, and we must earn it..... Whatever You say. I know there's a crucial time between now and October..... I know You have great plans, and Butchie said His love is my first mission, Father, and in loving Him and in being with Him always, and not allowing people to steal my time away from Him, then my mission will be a success before Thee.....

Nope, that's all I want, Father. I'll do anything You want, and if loving Butchie , and devoting all my attention to Him is the key to Your victory, Father, then that's the way it will be..... If You want me to, I will..... Yes..... I'm listening Father..... **"You see, Eileen, I have called You to a very important and powerful mission. I will give you all the graces you need to accomplish this mission, a mission that will give God's Church back to His people."**

What's God's Church, Father, the Roman Catholic Church?..... **The Church of love**..... Father, I don't mean to question You, but you know I'm a Roman Catholic. I can't just say "Church of love," can I, Father?..... **I can, under Roman Catholicism, Father, for that's where You want me to stand. They will see all the love that comes**

from the Father and the Son. Yes, with pride I will walk through it, Father, but with justice and balance through doctrine and tradition. And they will see that I am founded on the love of my Father, my Spouse Butchie, and the light of the Holy Spirit.

But how will I change it, Father?..... *(laughs)* I remember that story about the pea under the mattress. *(laughs)* I remember it well..... Then I will be the pea that brings back the sensitivity of Mother Church *(laughs).* You're funny. I love it, Father, I love it for sure.....

That sounds real beautiful. That sounds promising, Father. **Before You call me to the kingdom, the Church will rise gloriously once again**..... That makes me feel so good, it makes me feel like crying..... That sounds real important. I hope I never let You down my Father. It sounds so important, so big.....

(laughs) I don't know about a masterpiece. I just delight hearing You say it, Father. I love You so much. I want to do everything You want me to do. I love being with You all the time. I hate being tied down to the earth, and yet to do Your will makes me so happy, Father. It makes me happy that You have chosen me to do something for You. It thrills me to death that You have chosen me, Father..... Of all the smart and beautiful and intelligent and skilled people, *(laughs)* You came down to a scullery maid, making her queen for a day..... I feel important, and yet I feel humbled. I don't know exactly how I feel, except I love You so much, Father, and I'm so happy that I'm able to do something. I want to do everything that You want me to do.....

No, it just makes me feel like I'm running towards You faster, and makes me feel like I want to accomplish it fast, as fast as I can, and as perfect as I can, so I can be with You forever..... I'm going to hold You to that promise, Father, You can't lie, You know, You're God..... *(laughs)* For sure. I just thought I should remind You.....

A little vessel, I love that part so much..... I understand that. I know Carsha will be with me. It's very important..... I'm listening to everything..... You said that once before to me, "the white stallion of faith"..... **In this life that I shall lead, I shall touch many souls.** They'll be better, Father?..... I understand the time is getting short. I feel that, Father..... No sadness at all, the only thing I want to do is to come to see You. But I'll remember this, my Father. I will teach them Your words through Carsha. I will reach out to them with love, and they will only be part of my life through prayer. No one, but no one must enter my life, because now there is real work ahead..... **All work is important, but the most important work lies before me.** I understand, Father..... I'm excited, wondering, but not afraid. How can I be afraid when You are with me, Father? The only time I'm afraid is when You take a powder with Butchie during Lent. Then I'm scared to death..... I know You are there, Father, even then.

PART TWO: SOULS – LOST AND GAINED

SO MANY!

October 17, 1984

I know that You love me. What brought this on, Butchie ?..... What do You want to show me?..... Step out of my valley, for what reason?..... All right, You do the leading, and I will follow You..... It's a ledge *[they are standing on, looking down].* What are they? They look like leaves, but instead they're lights..... I don't know..... What do You mean?..... I notice they look like lights instead of leaves. They begin like hazy white lights and then they turn gray and then black and they are falling and falling and falling. Where are they falling to?..... What?.....

Butchie, that many? That many? Can't You do something about it? Can't we do something about it? I can't believe it. I can't believe it. It's like a wind blowing the leaves from the trees. I can't believe this. So many, Butchie. It's unbelievable. I hurt awful. Why are You showing this to me?..... Butchie, why do they begin with the white haze and then become gray and then black?..... **All of them reject grace.**

But how can we change it?..... **We can't change the ones that are falling, but we can prevent others from falling.....** No, there is no way to glue the leaves back to a tree. They are gone, until a new life springs forth next year..... Well, then they die and fall to the ground.....

What has that got to do with souls?..... **And You need, You want sacrifices.** Why are You showing this to me, Butchie, today?..... **One of the Father's greatest pains.....** I know He won't interfere with free will, but couldn't He inspire us to pray more for those sinners to change them? I can't bear to think that so many are lost. Stop them from falling, do something..... I know the Father won't interfere with free will. But there must be something we can do..... **Pray.** Is prayer enough?..... **Sacrifice. But some will always be lost.** I can't believe it. I can't believe it.

Like the leaves falling from the trees, Butchie. You paid the price, yet so many..... But why are You showing this to me today?..... I never realized so many. I can't bear to look any more. I don't want to look any more..... Yes, I want to go back.....

Well, of course I am sad. Look what You showed me..... I understand. I am listening well..... I can't believe it. I can't believe it. I know what You say is true, but I am shocked. I know we aren't saints. I know we are sinners, and I know we repent, but so many lost forever! I can't believe it. It's hard to understand my Father's mercy and His justice. It's hard. I know He's the merciful Father, and then I remember His justice. It's hard for me to balance it, Butchie. Why do You do this to me? Why now?...... .

In the last six months there have been more souls lost than in the last two thousand years. I don't want to hear this, Butchie. I come to You to be joyful, to be loved by You, to have peace, and You place this before me. Why now?.....

I know about Capi..... I know. But why now? Why?..... **It's a struggle between body and soul, between man and God and the evil one. It's like a tug of war with the Father. The Father is trying to get us into the kingdom, and Capi is trying to pull us out..... .**

But how can I stop them? I don't understand. You are showing this to me for a reason, but I don't understand..... I'm listening, but a part of me seems like it died. I am in shock. It's unreal. I won't hold the Father's words back, if it meant every night, I would do it, Butchie ..... If I am, it's because of Carsha. I will do whatever Carsha says, whatever You wish, Butchie ..... How would You do that?..... Yes, that does make me feel better.

I just can't seem to grasp it. With all the preaching in the world, all the gifted people, and all the people reaching out, this is still happening. It is hard for me to understand. But what about Mary's apparitions, and still this is happening? I am confused. I'm confused..... Yes, I preach Your words, whatever the Father wants me to preach..... No, only for the Father's glory. That's my only reward.

Preaching has become a fast money-making act..... Even the preachers will fall. I don't feel like I want to preach any more, Butchie.

. You scare me to death..... Maybe I don't want to be scared to life..... It's a responsibility, a big responsibility..... All I want them to do is to love the Father, to know You, Butchie, and to know Carsha.....

That's what I tell them. To love You more than You've been loved. I want my people to love You. I want to love You the most. I know You are trying to cheer me and make me feel good, but I'm hurting awful, hurting awful..... Well, because You paid such a price for them. You have to do something, Butchie. The Father must hurt awful. I wish I knew where His justice began and ended and His mercy and love...... We remember His love and His mercy, we forget His justice. Darn old justice.....

I don't know. When I think of His justice, sometimes I get frightened of my Father. Sure I love Him so. I know its not Him. It's us. Yes, I felt His majesty, His power, His greatness, but I felt His love. But this really scares me, Butchie.

Father, it frightens me to see those souls falling into hell. I don't mean to upset You, Father, but for a moment I was afraid of You, my Father, afraid of Your justice..... I know You didn't put them there. They put themselves..... I know of Your mercy, Father, and I know of Your love. But at this moment, my Father, I am afraid of Your justice. I know I wouldn't do anything against Thee, but You love them like You love me and look where they're going.....

I understand that, Father, but still I am scared. I try to walk in Carsha's light and never hurt You, my Father..... But do they really know, do they understand what they are coming to?..... You said You would use the time to save them, I remember..... **But they wouldn't accept the time.....**

My Father, I believe You gave them every opportunity..... Then take this fear from my heart, my Father. I don't want fright to be between us. Please take it away, my Father. I know it's not from You. I remember the threads, Father *{He looks for a thread to save a soul]*, and that it's easy *[to be saved]*.....

I do believe You're hurting, my Father..... Yes, I do believe You gave them every chance. There's no doubt in my mind about that,

Father..... It's my humanness that gets frightened. Why all this now? What do You ask from me? What can I do?..... I do that, Father. I'm trying to do the best I can. I listen to Carsha and I preach Your words, Father.....

Call My people together to be holy people, walking and living in the light of the Holy Spirit. Call my priests..... But I don't think they are all running here..... I know the Church is in trouble. I fear for my Church, my Father, but I don't know what else to do but to pray. I know I am self-centered and I'm thinking how much I hurt over this, but I know You must hurt even more, Father, and I am so sorry for thinking of me. I should be easing Your pain.

I know how much You love these souls. It's such a shock to me, but it's heartbreaking to You, Father. I'm so sorry..... I can't say that yet, Father, because I still fear..... I want to but I'm fearful. I know You want to hear it, Father, but I would be lying. Please help me, take the fear from me, my Father. It's the most horrible thing I ever saw.

They knew, they knew, and yet they would not change. I understand at least a little of Your hurt..... I understand that, Father. I need Your help with this. I don't love You less, no, of course not. I love You more, because You are hurting more than I am hurting, but it's that justice that scares me..... It's lighter than it was before, Father, but it still scares me, and I don't want anything about You to frighten me, Father. Help me with this please, my Father. Please help me with this fear.....

I know I preach You're all just and holy, but I also preach You're all merciful and all love. I need help with it, Father..... Yes, I see it before me. **I must preach about the mercy and love of my Father for his children and also his justice.....** Of course I will do as You say, but I need Your love ever so much, Father. I need Your love more than ever now. It's the first time I've ever feared You, and that fear alone is enough to floor me, Father.....

I know You didn't. I never experienced it before, Father. I know You love me..... I understand that, Father. I do love You beyond all human understanding. I can't even understand all this love I feel for You. Not that You're not worthy of it for sure, but You place this love in my heart. Have You placed this fear?..... Why, Father? **To give to Your people.** But do You want them to fear You, Father? I thought You want them to love You..... **Love You to a point of fearing to ever hurt You.** That sounds better. Love You to a point of fearing and dreading to ever hurt You. Thank You, Father.....

My Father speaks truths. I don't have fear of Your love, nor of Your mercy. I fear Your justice..... **If I walk in the light of Carsha, then justice should be a joy for me.** Why do I shake, why do these fingers grasp my heart then if it should be joyful?..... **Because in justice when I do the right thing, there will be a just reward, the kingdom, my valley.**

Then I should rejoice rather than fear..... **The only ones who should fear Your justice are those who walk away from You.** Then why did I just feel fear, Father? Am I not walking in Your love, in Your light?..... Then why shouldn't I feel joy in Your justice? Why do I feel fear?..... **Because I love souls, and to see them lost causes me pain.....**

I am not fearing Your justice. What am I fearing?..... **Loss of those souls.** That sounds better, and I can feel the hurt releasing. If I walk straight in Your love and love You, my Father, and do Your will, then Your justice will be a joy to me and not a painful thing. I can feel the pain lifting, Father. I can understand more clearly Your justice.....

I love You too. I love You so much, Father. It's the first time I ever felt that fear, but now I understand it, Father, and it's erased from me. I never want to feel it again..... Thank You, Father, it has passed from me.

A FIELD FULL OF FLOWERS

October 24, 1984

No, now it's my turn. Let me make one for You...... Maybe it won't be as beautiful as the one you made for me, but at least I will try to make one, Butchie. *(laughs)* There now, see, You look handsome. We'll look in the brook and You'll see how great You look..... I know, but You are every inch a man.....

Don't we look good together?..... For ever and ever..... Thank You..... I love You too. Come on let's walk through the water. Now don't show off, get Your feet wet. *(laughs)* Remember when I pushed You in? It wasn't too many years ago. *(laughs)* Will I cross to the other side?..... They're already dry.....

It's so peaceful here. I'm so happy here. I love it here, Butchie . Thank You for my crown. It's beautiful, and You look mighty handsome in Yours..... Forever. You mean for all eternity? *(laughs)*.....

I just want to sit here and enjoy this grass and these flowers, Butchie. I enjoy that brook so much. *(laughs)* Remember when we were courting. I said I didn't want to grow up and You rippled the water to make me look wrinkled and You said, Now you're grown up..... I remember everything we did together..... Nothing seems to bother me here.....

No, it's been a real rough week..... No, not just that, Butchie. Other things, but I don't want to get into it, to spoil this time together. I love the fields and I love the smell of the flowers and the air is so clean and the brook is so clear and everything loves everything.

You know what I was wondering, in those Life in the Spirit seminars, I thought it was the light of the Spirit, but I don't know, You'll have to help me. The charismatic movement was so happy and so joyful. I meant to ask You this before. Were they getting the light of the Spirit? Was it just a movement?..... **There was some light of the Holy Spirit leading them to communicate with the Father, nature and all His creations, but it didn't have the strength**

of baptism. Is that what it was?..... There is so much strength in baptism, right. I didn't want today to be a day of teaching, just a day of relaxing, but You have a way of teaching me, Butchie.

It's funny I can smell it for sure, even though with my cold I can't smell anything.....

Don't be silly. I don't know how much I love You. I love You as much as I can, I guess..... I don't know. How can I measure that? I'm not the Son of the Father. Only You can do that. You are so serious at times.....

I promise I will. They're beautiful. Each one is so unique. I'm afraid to let You go behind the tree because I never know if You are going to come back or what You are up to. I'll come with You..... You're silly..... More than anything in the whole world.....

Where did You get them?..... You picked them before I came. They are so beautiful, and You're so beautiful. Each time I see You I love You more. I appreciate You more..... Now what am I going to put these in? They're so beautiful..... It's just like a vase, a standing vase. When I come they'll still be in the tree?..... **Anything You give to me will last forever.** And I will come and I'll look for that bouquet. I will remember that You gave them to me. The tree is hugging the flowers, saying, I'll keep them until you get here.

Why are You so loving, what are You up to?..... Yes, You're always loving to me, but when You are extra loving and extra kind, You're up to something..... Yes, I trust You. I just want to know what You are up to..... **Love.** You know I trust Your love, but still I want to know what You are up to..... *(laughs)* Is that what I sound like?

I feel safe here. Nothing can get to me and pull me down..... That's our song. We walked in the meadows, You were my big brother. "Now we've grown to an adult size." I remember that well..... When You talk like this, Butchie, I feel so loved. I feel as though I could go through anything just to get to You.....

My love grows with pain. I have to think about that for a minute. My love grows with pain..... Well I'm not too bright. I have to let it sink in. It means the pain and suffering of the world makes my love grow deeper for You, Butchie. You like to mess up my hair too. What is it about my hair that makes everybody want to mess it up?.....

Well, I'm glad wonderful things are going to happen when I come, but I would like wonderful things to happen now..... Well, lots of stuff. I would like to see my church filled and people growing closer to the Father. I wish I could tell them about my valley, how we walk together and play together, how alive You really are. You just fill me with love.....

Hi, my Father. Of course I'm happy. I love to be here and I'm happy because I'm here. I'd love to be here permanently..... I'm not going to talk about that now..... Loads of stuff. We've been walking through the water..... Do You like Jesus' crown? I made it for Him out of flowers, my Father. Butchie gave flowers to me and we stuck them in the tree and the tree just seems to love to hold them. It's going to take care of them for me until I come forever.....

You will? You will give me a whole field of flowers. For me?..... **You will allow me to pick them and throw them to earth.** Won't they die when they are out of my valley?..... You mean when I throw them they will turn into graces and blessings, the whole field full, Father? I bet my friends will love that. We need blessings, Father. I'm glad You're going to turn them into blessings. They wouldn't know the color of these flowers. But a whole field full, Father, and more so?..... **The moment I breathe my last breath.** I wish we could do it now. Maybe we could change everybody, including myself. I don't know how You think of these beautiful things, Father. I couldn't think of them in a million years..... **A field full of flowers will be picked and sent to earth to all the people.** There are so many here. You're so kind to us and so wonderful. I love You so much, my Father.

I would like one of those blessings now, Father. I'm not asking for a special privilege, but to send it down to earth, so that we may have peace...... You're so wonderful, Father, I love You so much.....

That's the most beautiful thing You have given to me, Father. All Your gifts are wonderful. I just can't wait..... More than anything in the world..... That makes me feel good. Your hand is so warm and so gentle, yet I feel its firmness and love. There is no shadow of a doubt that I am Yours, my Father.

THE GREATEST LOVE STORY

Nov. 11, 1984

Why don't You hold my hand? You lead me to the tree..... You're always filled with surprises..... Oh no, not You too!..... I don't like it, but do I have a choice?..... No, You never have. You told me stories before but You never read to me. So I guess I can take it for a little while. I just hope You don't start preaching to me, Butchie, or reading from books. I'm going to tell the Father if You do because I don't like that stuff..... Yep, I'm comfortable..... Yep, You have my attention. I'm listening, Butchie. Butchie, I've heard so many things about them. All right I won't interrupt any more. But if I fall asleep it is Your fault.....

No, don't stop. I want to hear some more. I'll let You know when I get bored. I'm listening..... No, that makes me feel good. To know that I live in such a time for sure. I like to hear about the good people..... Oh, I don't know. I like Ralph Martin, is this about him?..... I like Mother Basilea, is this about her?..... Well they are two of the best people I know..... I'm listening, I'm listening..... Yes, I am interested. At least right now. I don't know if I'll be interested in a little while, but now I am.....

Nope, don't stop, I want to hear some more..... Nope, it sounds special to me..... Yes, I do want to listen. Go ahead, I'll let You know.....

That's it! I don't want to hear any more! No more, that's it..... No more, Butchie, no more.

Let me see it. You are so funny. Does the Father know what You are doing? I'm going to tell Him. You got me interested for a while, my Friend. Then You gave it away, Butchie.

Come on, let's go down by the brook. Put that book away. Come on with me, Butchie, let's go see the fishes..... I don't want to hear the rest of it..... Good! I'm glad its Your masterpiece. Now You read it to Yourself. Lets go see the fish.....

You're funny. I love You because You are so cute and so funny.

Leave the book, You look like a scholar. Come on, let's go.....

I love You too, Butchie, and I love everything You do. But sometime You are so nutty..... I don't know about that. Come on, let's go. Your silly face and mine..... You sure do..... You're so funny.....

I know all about Romeo and Juliet..... I do. I think our love story is far superior to theirs. It's different..... I certainly do think it's the greatest love story ever. But we are prejudiced.

Look at him. What's his name.... You remember every one of their names. He said, "Butchie, knock it off and give me some attention. Put that book down and pay attention to me." Yep. I'm saying that too..... Look at them, they are all saying, "Yes"..... **They know that I'm part of this valley. It's mine.** Although there are no bosses. We're just friends and loving one another..... **They know that I belong here, and that's why they swim so joyfully when I'm here. That's why the birds sing so beautiful when I'm here. They know I belong here.** Not in authority, in love, Butchie.....

Anything You ask, I'll answer if I can, You know my mind. I do, Butchie..... I have so many things coming up. I just want to do one at a time. I have the Priests' Day, Butchie. I'm nervous about that. I want to do my Father's will and draw them ever so close to the Father.

I don't know how much time I have left, but I want them to fall so much in love with You, Butchie, and the Father and Carsha. I don't know how many days or weeks or months or years that I have. Maybe there are a lot or maybe there are few, but I must use them.....

I think some spiritual people will understand it, but I don't know if everyone will understand it. Ask the Father.....

Father, You are so funny. I love You so much. If my wish is Your command, then how come You didn't let me win the Megabucks?..... I want to go to the kingdom for sure. There is no comparison, my Father, no comparison at all *[between going to the kingdom and winning the Megabucks]*.....

We're not up to much. Butchie was telling me that the fish swim joyfully and seem to be so happy when I'm here, my Father. I know You call it my valley, but I know there is no authority here, Father, except Yours. I know they are happy when I'm here. The birds are happy to have me listen to them. Even the flowers are happy when I give them attention.....

Ask Him what He has under his arm. He was reading it to me, my Father..... Oh, I liked it very much, my Father, it caught my interest in the beginning. You know I don't like to have anyone read to me. I don't like to read myself, but I became interested in it, real interested, until I knew whom it was about...... No I think it's the greatest love story ever. For sure, Father. Three great love stories. Falling in love with Butchie, falling in love with You, my Father. And the love I hold for Carsha..... **You could never print that.** You're as funny as Your Son..... You do! I'm happy about that Father. I never doubted it for a moment. At times my head swirls for sure. I don't think anyone has ever been so loved.....

Oh, I don't know, I could be very humble or try to be humble, and say I don't deserve it. But I truly expect Your love, and the love of Butchie, I would be lost without it. You spoiled me from the beginning.

Even when I don't hear it, Father, I know it's there..... No. I reached the point in my illness where nothing else matters *[i.e. in her terminal illness she resigned her family and children into His hands]*. I love to grow closer to You, Father. To draw so close to You and then leave them *[in Your hands]*, Father. *[To follow my family]* only by prayer..... For sure. I said I was worried about that. I know You always come through and Carsha comes through. But I guess it is because I'm human and You made me a human, so I worry. Do You mind me worrying?..... (laughs) **You worry too.**

GENDER AND THE DIVINE PERSONS

November 28, 1994

Maybe I am and maybe I am not. But You're reading things on my face..... I understand that. I know You are in control, but I still worry..... No, it's not the ministry this time, Butchie. I'm worried about her. I know, it's still in my humanness. I worry because she's so small. You wouldn't want me to be any other way, would You? I am her grandmother and I should worry, right?..... No, it's not to a point of mistrust. They both need Your help, the baby so she won't cry, and Colleen *[Eileen's daughter and the mother of baby Samantha]*, so she won't worry..... Yes, I trust You..... No, not to a point of losing my peace, but I do worry for sure. I'll feel better when she is home..... I know, it seems like there is always something to upset the apple cart, Butchie. The dog, the baby, always something.....

I would like her there, of course I would. She would take care of her just like she took care of You when You were a little boy. And I trust the Father..... No, I don't want to worry, because when I worry my head aches so bad. I am happy about everything..... Of course I am. Only because the Father's word will be out, and that makes me happy.

I'm wondering why all these doors are opening all of a sudden. Are You rushing a little?..... No, I'd be happy. I'd be so happy. The Father's word will be getting out and I'll be getting closer to being here forever.....

All I want to be is still and listen..... I say that over and over again, Butchie. I like to be here where it's quiet..... Nope, it seems the moment I make the resolution the phone rings right off the wall..... She has been answering it. I want to get back to the Father. I was talking about the Father's gifts. It's not so much the gifts, it's the mystery of it all. It's in quietness that the Father can do with me *[whatever He wants]*, Butchie. I just can't seem to have any peace. I believe You, I believe the Father is really working hard.....

No, I am not worried about that. I'm sure the Father through Carsha will give me the right words to say to them..... At first I hesitated, a long trip *[to Philadelphia]* for just thirty or fifty people..... But they are leaders, Butchie. I don't know. You know better than I do. I know they have some faith.....

I can see it unfolding now. It's like a jig saw puzzle. I can't quite put it together. I know He has a plan.....

Of course I trust You. It is right and I'm not..... Nope, I'm not putting down Carsha, I love Carsha. I will trust in His light.....

See, You say "He" for the Holy Spirit. You say "He" and I say "He." See that, then it's "He." It's the first time I heard You say of the Holy Spirit, "He." You used to say "the Spirit." Not "She." The Spirit, Carsha, is a "He," right?..... **There is no gender.....**

Mary is very definitely feminine, tender and gentle.....

I want You to go through that with me again, why You call the Spirit "He"....

That's right. He walked towards me with arms and legs, although I could not identify His face. He entered into a wedlock. God is not a contradiction.

I'm glad You are teaching me, because I have a great love for Carsha.

I think they look for new trips and they don't look for solid teaching from You, Butchie. They are looking for eery things. They don't stop to realize what You're all about. I guess I couldn't stop either. It's because You help me, so I don't blame them for that. But I can't understand that they say the Spirit is "She." Even without You saying "He," it was the light that made me say "He."

I know, it's not like a *[human]* birth, it's the power of all the forces of love forming another person. The power rather than the genes, right?..... I'm pretty sure I grasped it, but I don't know if I could explain it so somebody else could grasp it. They'll think I am crazy. I don't know if I dare get into it. As long as I know what You say, it is all right by me..... **It's not like a human birth from a mother.**

It's the birth from power. I think that's super. It is so easy *[to understand]*.

Sometimes You make me understand things so easily, Butchie, and sometimes I just can't..... I'm sure it is Him. I will write it in my book..... I can't give it to them unless Carsha gives me the light, nor would I dare. But I'll be open to everything You and the Father want to teach me..... Carsha will give me the light to understand, but for *[receiving]* teaching I need silence. Help me to have it, Butchie. Please help me to have my silence. I want it more than anything in the world. People don't understand it. I love them and I give myself to them, but I want to be quiet with my Jesus, with my Father, and with Carsha. I want to know everything You want to teach me.....

Well that depends upon You. I'll cooperate if You help me..... Yes, I do want to get all those teachings. They are deep. This one about Carsha is very deep. I have to think about it.

I trust You, sure. I know what You say is true. It is amazing why they try to do this. It's because they are liberals, right? Well, I don't even want to mention that stuff in my talks. They'll string me up. I don't want to get into a political debate with them.

I would rather tell them how gentle and loving a mother is and how we can imitate her, and how our husbands adore us when we are like this, not when we act like men. I'm sure we can do it, Butchie..... I will, I'll write down everything You and my Father tell me.....

Yes, it's very important because the teachings are going to be very deep. But You'll teach them to me, right? You'll make me understand. I don't want to mix them up..... Yes, I know, I must have my peace. I long for it so much I ache.

Well, I ache for my peace, Father. Butchie said You are going to give me some profound teachings now and I must write them down. But I need silence to grasp them and peace and quiet to hear them, my Father..... But You must help me too. Father, I love You so much..... **In the stillness of my heart I find the gift of *[my]* nothingness.** I must be still again, Father.

The moment I make a resolution to have it everything's thrown at me, everything. It's unbelievable..... I trust You. I love You so much, Father. I know You're opening these doors for me and I want to do Your will, and only Your will, and I want Carsha to help me through these doors because I know I can't do it alone. But my Father, I want my silence back.

Father, this morning at Eucharist with Butchie, I prayed for that silence, I need it now. I ache for it like I ache for the kingdom. Please help me, Father..... **You put that desire in my heart.** Then help me fulfill it, Father..... You said the desire isn't enough, then You better help me, Father.

Butchie told me about Carsha. I don't know if I could explain it, but I know what He means. They misinterpret the word "Bridegroom" in Scripture..... If You tell me I could make a tape on the "Bridegroom" and what it means, Father. There's a lot more to it.

I believe we fall in love with Jesus as a brother, as a friend..... See, You are teaching me already. I don't think You have to do any more tonight. These things are deep, my Father, I don't want a headache. You better wait awhile. I could think of it all week.....

There is so much You want to reveal to the world. Then You better reveal it, Father. We could really use it.....

I'd like that. Say it again, Father. **"Come Child and I will open My kingdom to thee. I will reveal the secrets of the kingdom, and you will whet the appetites of the souls of My people. What they will hear will make them hunger and thirst after the Lord. And they will know that you speak the truth".....**

More than anything in the whole world. Why do You think I beg so much to come? Why do You think I get almost angry when someone else goes to You ahead of me? I feel cheated. And yet I know I have work to do. And then sometimes I think I have not suffered enough. I will suffer more.....

Well, either way it's suffering. And then I think that I've been naughty, I need to suffer and it quiets my soul. I figure I am getting what I deserve, and I am being purified, and then my soul settles down, my Father.....

I love You too. I love You so much I can't even put it into words, my Father......

No, I want everyone to love You, but I'm selfish, I want to love You the best and the most. I want to be the only one that pats Your cheeks and pinches Your nose. I want them to love You. But I want to have special privileges, Father..... Right....

"THEY'RE ONLY GETTING ONE STATION"

1985 Otherwise undated. Day after rock festival for African relief

I think what they did was beautiful *[the rock festival for African relief which drew an estimated crowd of 35,000 people]*, and I think it's going to help lots of people. Half of them had no voices at all. They acted like clowns and stupid. What must we do to bring them to my Father's house, Butchie?.....

Why don't we fill the church?..... Oh, You know better than I that you could barely understand the words. What is wrong, Butchie, what can I do? This is my heaviest burden. I don't know what I can do to draw them to the Father's house......

Well, look how long it took me to get this far. I don't have that much time left, at least I don't think I do..... *(laughs)* No, I'm not trying to bribe You into telling me. Oh Butchie, what's wrong, what are we lacking?.....

I'm patient but I guess I'm impatient. That church should be filled. Look at all the people and children who turned up *[for the rock festival]*. I'm sure the youth didn't turn up just for Africa. They turned out to listen to all those top bands..... **Much good was drawn out of it.** Sure, but why can't we do this, Butchie?

I just can't get it out of my mind. What's wrong with us? I don't know what else I can do to draw more in closer and deeper. What else can I do, Butchie?..... That's not a good answer, I am myself. What can I do?.....

My heart was broken. They can draw the people in with their craziness, and we can't draw them in for the love of the Father. Butchie, please help me..... No, I just want them to come to the Father's house to hear His word. Can't we turn them on to the Father, as they're turned on to all this music? What is the magic they have, Butchie, that we don't have?.....

There's something wrong..... I know, but is that enough, Butchie? **Those that hear you come back.** But why can't we draw more? It seems like we're slighting the Father. We're lacking something,

Butchie, we're lacking lots of stuff. Please help me.....

Yes, **they are responding**, Butchie, but not enough, not enough. Why can't we turn them on to You, to Carsha, to my Father?..... Well, it is depressing me. I feel like I'm short changing the Father. Butchie help me to find out what it is. And tell Carsha to give me what I need to draw these people in.....

Yes, **they come to hear.** But look at those priests in Springfield right next door *[to Worcester]*. They never even heard of me..... I was thinking yesterday, if all that shouting and yelling and that screaming and that laughing was given to the Father, just imagine how happy You would be. That bothered me all day yesterday.....

Father, it was the crowds that bothered me, not you, Father. I know it was a good cause. I'm sure those that paid so much money for the tickets weren't thinking just of the good cause. They were thinking of the top bands that were going to be there. And good was coming from this and good will still come from it, Father, and I accept that. But what kills me is why we can't draw them to You, Father. I lack something, and I need Your help, my Father.....

Of course You know what I was thinking, Father, 'cause You're God. Picture You on that stage with all Your children..... I was trying to imagine how You would feel. All the glory when the Son walks off and hears the screams of the people.

They were doing good. I understand that. I'm not knocking that, Father. But why can't we do this for the Trinity? It's because we're lacking something and I want to know how I can do better, Father. This glory should be directed towards You, my Father..... I know You know what I was thinking, if it all could have been directed to Your praise and worship. 90 million people *[in the T.V. audience]*. How You would shower graces and blessings upon Your children in this land.

Father, my heart is hurting about this. I have to do something about this, Father. I know it's You who have placed this heavy upon my heart. I need help, Father. Tell me what to do and get Carsha moving in this direction..... I know. I do think of the positive things *[that are happening]*, but You're the positive thing in my life, my Father. And I want all this attention to go to You, Father. I really don't know what else to do, Father, to draw them on my Sunday. I feel like I've come to a blank wall, especially after seeing that yesterday.....

No, no, I only feel sad, Father, to the point that You should be getting all this glory, all this attention, and no one turns out..... **It's filling,** Father, but it should be filled by now. There's something You must help me with Father, please..... I know that, Father. They say it over and over again that **once they come to me they never want to miss it.** But why aren't the rest coming, Father?..... But what can I do?..... Yes, I believe they are doing a lot and this retreat will help. And the Conference will help. But I want it to blossom here, Father *[at the fourth Sunday service at St. John's church]*.....

I don't know what to do..... But is that enough? Are You happy with that?..... I believe You, but I'm not happy with it, so I don't agree with You. I'm not happy at all with it, not after seeing yesterday. I'll have to fill that church to overflowing *[to be satisfied]*. I want the praise and the worship for You to blow the roof right off the church, Father.....

I'm listening, Father..... It's hard not to be discouraged. It's been a long time, Father..... You are not discouraged?..... Yes, I understand that, but I love You so much, Father. It kills me..... **You're their God, You're their Father, they have to understand this.** But why can't we get the message across? What's the blockage, Father?..... And is that the biggest blockage? **They get but one station. They are only getting the station of the things of this world. And all they have to do is turn the knob to another station and they'll get the Father.**

But can't we help them out, Father? Look how long it took me..... I know discouragement never comes from You, Father. But I can't help but feeling it at times. I was telling Butchie all I could picture was You sitting on that stage, with Your hands raised in blessing over all these children who had come to see You.....

It was good they couldn't understand the words. Their gestures were stupid and you couldn't tell whether they were girls or boys, Father. You have to help me turn the knob to the station, then, to get them tuned into the Father..... I've waited a long time Father. I know Your time is different, but I get discouraged..... If you say so, Father. Please have Carsha help me to do what I can to draw them closer to You, Father..... Is that true? **If they come to You, they have a responsibility to fulfill what they have heard.** I still want them to come, Father.....

Yes, the priests and the bishops are saying it's a good crowd, but it's not enough, Father, not for You, Father. We should outdo these music groups, and I don't know where to begin..... They love Your teachings. They've opened up to the healings.....

I hope I do, Father. That's all I want to do, to reflect You. I love You so much. I wanted You to be there, visible to them. And I want them to come to see You, to hear Your word. **We just can't drag them in.....** I trust You, Father..... I believe it, because You say it. I believe whatever You say. I may not feel it inside right now, but I know I'll feel it by grace.....

Really, then You know, and I know You know, what I was thinking. It really pleased You, Father?..... **They have to come by faith; they have to be drawn by faith. You could visibly pop onto the stage and then they'd know You are God. But this isn't the way You want to draw them. You want to draw them by their faith, by my reflecting You.**

But, Father, they have to hear about me first. Look, right over the border *[of the diocese]*, they haven't even heard of me. They had to go to Philadelphia to hear about me. There's something stinky in Denmark..... *(laughs)* I love it, but tell me again..... **"The greatest gift I received from all over the world was the pain in your heart wishing I were getting all that praise and glory."** That was the gift to You, Father?..... Was I lamenting like Jeremiah? Really, my Father, You took it as the great gift from Eileen? And You know I meant it with all my heart. I wanted You to be there, the center of everything and the praise and worship giving You glory. I'm so happy You accepted it as a gift, Father. That makes me feel better. And this is my greatest gift to be here with You. To have You hold me so close and to love me, Father. They don't know what they are missing..... I hope we will, Father. I hope so. **"Be not afraid, I go before thee,"** then I won't be afraid 'cause You'll be there.

1. Bishop Daniel P. Reilly (then Bishop of Norwich, now of Worcester) with priests
at Eileen's annual Priests Retreat in Putnam, CT September 1990

2. Eileen with Anthony Cardinal Bevilacqua at the Catholic Charismatic Conference in Philadelphia, June 1988

3. Eileen with Bishop James McHugh of Camden at a Charismatic Conference
Credit: Joseph P. Barrett

4. Eileen with Archbishop George Pearce, S.M. and priest retreatants at Eileen's annual Priests' Retreat, Putnam, CT. September 21, 1994 Credit: Bill Splaine

5. Priests with Eileen at a St. Joseph's-in-the-Hills, Malvern, PA retreat

6. Eileen with retreatants in Assisi, Italy

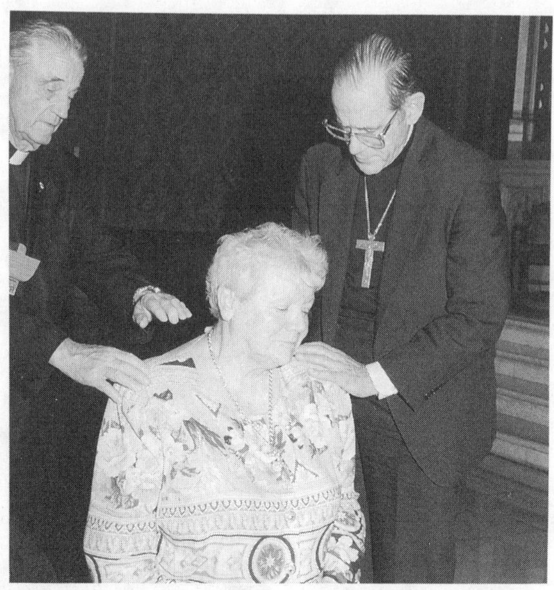

7a Archbishop Pearce, SM and Fr. J.B.Palm, SJ of Taiwan praying over Eileen before a service at Sts. Peter and Paul Cathedral, Providence, RI

7b Fr. Paul Wiericha, CP, Director of Bishop Molloy Retreat Center, Jamaica, NY with Eileen May 1996

8a Bishop Thomas J. Welsh of Allentown with Eileen May 15, 1996

8b. Bishop M. Pearse Lacey, Auxiliary BishopEmeritus of Toronto with Eileen June 5, 1996

9. Eileen's appreciative retreatants at St. Joseph-in-the-Hills Retreat House, Malvern, PA, September 1986 Credit: Bill Splaine

10. Msgr. Vincent Walsh and Eileen at the Catholic Charismatic Conference in Philadelphia, June 1988. Credit: G. Butler/Omega

PART THREE: GOD–LOVE

GETTING GOD-LOVE STRAIGHT

January 16, 1985

Butchie, I think I'm the only one in the whole world that knows that You dance with me. You're so light on Your feet. You don't look like a dancer *[in likenesses]*..... I don't know. Probably You look like You have Your nose to the plow of religion. We bypass the joyful God..... I don't know if they would love You more. I think they would be able to relate to You more..... But would they understand what we do?..... Oh no, I enjoy it so much. You glide over the flowers, never brushing them..... As light as a feather..... Forever and ever.....

The world knows you as a loving Son, a good Son, a prayerful Son, a Son who sacrificed His life for His people. But they just don't know this side of You, Butchie. That You laugh and that You love and that You dance and that You talk.....

(cough) You're lucky You're immune to my germs..... See how You spoil me, and then You wonder why I don't want to go back. I bring with me my faults, my coughs, my germs, even my temper..... **They'll be gone when I stay here forever.** See Butchie, if only they knew You as I know You. All the things we did together growing up, our love-time together, our dancing together..... But there are things that I can't tell them. Not that I can't, but they wouldn't accept them. They might even say I was irreverent.....

The nun said it, You know *[a sister said that she was irreverent calling Jesus "Butchie"]*. I'm not afraid of what they say, but I don't want to spoil the Father's work.....

Every time we come there is more beauty...... I don't know. Sometimes I compare You to an artist. You keep touching things up to make them look more beautiful for me. And the flowers seem brighter, and the birds sing more beautifully. The fishes look better. So every time I come it's a new awakening. And You look more beautiful than ever.....

Everything seems to be so loving and so in tune. The way You feel, the way You walk and the way You talk. Everything's in tune with everything else. No one's pulling one a different way. Peace just keeps flooding my soul......

There are so many things for me here. I want to be part of the valley forever, and when I leave I feel as though part of me is here. A part that never will come back to earth. And then, when I come here, it seems as though that part is united to me. It's like there are two parts of me, the spiritual and the human. I know my soul comes with me. So what's the explanation for this feeling?.....

The soul, the spirit, the body. Like the Father, the Son, and the Holy Spirit. My soul comes with me, as it must. I couldn't even breathe, nor walk, nor talk without it..... I thought the soul was the spirit, my spirit..... Then I have a spirit besides a soul..... Wait a minute, Butchie, back up. I don't understand it. Body and soul and spirit..... That's means I cannot separate the body and soul until the hour of death..... **My spirit can be here.....** Then won't I be lacking in something?..... I think I understand. If my Father's with me in my valley, my spirit's there. I call upon You and the Father on earth and You're there, and my spirit is there..... **My spirit is where my God is.....** This is difficult to understand, Butchie.....

I think I do, but it's a little bit difficult..... **My spirit belongs with my Father, my God.....** Your teachings are beautiful, Butchie, but they're so hard for me to grasp at times..... *(laughs)* Now You're a poet. Two minutes ago You were a singer..... *(long pause)* That's beautiful..... *(long pause)* That is really beautiful..... *(long pause)*

He's singing to me, Father. *(laughs)* You could hear Him?..... I love it. And I love the words, they're beautiful..... It makes me feel like He's turning a mushroom into a rose *(laughs)*..... Did You really like it, Father?..... I know sometimes I'm not the best company, but I just love being with You..... **In suffering, I run to You faster.....** I'm glad of that..... I always thought I ran to You for everything, not just with my suffering..... I'm happy about that, my Father..... **Suffering is an evil. Some souls have turned to You through suffering.** I know it's true, Father.....

(laughs) That's a good one..... I think hate is terrible. It's a terrible word, and I don't like it..... I like the word love..... **Love can be good and it can be dangerous.** More dangerous than hate, Father? How can love be more dangerous than hate?..... A lion? He could kill for his cub. Of course he loves his cub..... Is that what You mean?..... I understand, Father.

So it has to be the right kind of love. The love resting in the Father's heart. Right?..... **Human love is more dangerous than hate, but loving God is the love that we should have.....** When You put it that way, Father, I understand it..... You're a good teacher..... *(laughs)* I doubt that. But not that I doubt Your words. I don't know about me, I mean.....

You mean this year is more crucial than last? But we're going to make it better, Father, right?..... I don't like that word *popularity*, Father. We were talking about happy things. Why are You talking about this, Father..... **It fits in with love.....** Then they're not having the right love for the Father..... **They're having a love, but it's not the proper love of God. It's the love of themselves and their own prestige. And that's a destructive love.** That's why You're talking about it..... Everything You say is important to me.....

It's easy for You to say, Father, because You're God. It's hard for us to be like that, we're just human beings. You made us this way..... Nope, not that way, but You made us humans. You didn't put the faults there. But it's hard for us, Father..... **When man gets in the way, then You get out of the picture.** Then that means the real love is for God, and this naughty love is a destructive love, right?.....

And that's what's happening in the Church today, destructive love has replaced the divine..... Then we're destroying ourselves?..... Then how can we get back, Father? *(long pause)*..... But you hear so much about the basics of the Church, Father. I know what You mean, Father, but it's not that easy..... **Then if we don't get back to the true love, then we're going to destroy ourselves by destructive love, as the lion with the cub. We will kill, but it won't be for the love of the Father..... It'll be for self-esteem, to be popular, that's a bad love. A**

good love will keep his or her eyes on the Father. Care less what man thinks about her, but only what the Father sees in her.....

And the moment I start worrying about what people think, then I'm pushing Your love out, and letting the worldly love come in, which will destroy me..... Then we're not going to let it happen, right?..... I'm listening. I want to get straight what You're telling me..... I got God-love straight..... *(laughs)* I got Yours straight too, Butchie. I want to get these teachings straight.....

Then the Father's the goal, and that brings a pure, divine love into everything. There's no room for the destructive love that kills. It can destroy more than hatred does. They sound like the same to me..... No, they're not. I remember the lion loves the cub, but will kill for it. I'm not allowed to do that. The divine love won't kill for anything. Neither for pride, nor jealousy, nor envy, nor greatness..... I love being with You, even if we don't talk, just being with You – forever.

THERE IS NO [RELIGIOUS] EXPERIENCE WITHOUT LOVE

February 10, 1985

It's a wonderful surprise, Butchie, having Big Puppy here. You know how much I love Big Puppy *[a pet dog Eileen had for about 14 years before he disappeared].* It's the first time you brought him here to the valley. You love him, don't You, Butchie? Look at the way he looks at You..... I'm filled with peace over it..... Everything I love You put in my valley. And You can't blame me for wanting to come..... Nobody wants to hear about death, but to me it's life.....

It's so beautiful having Puppy here with us..... It seems like it's our favorite spot..... I don't know. A million thoughts race through my head. I don't know if I could pinpoint one. But so many things race through my mind when I'm here..... I think about how blessed I am being here. And then I want to share it with everybody.....

But how could I tell them such things? The peace and the tranquility. The love that I feel..... I do, Butchie, I really try to whet their appetites..... Most grasp it and are hungry for it..... I do see the wonderment in their faces..... No, honestly, Butchie, I didn't find one skeptic yet. I'm sure they're there, but I haven't found one..... They're so hungry for the kingdom..... At least to know about the kingdom, Butchie. And I don't know how much you want me to give them..... Carsha does inspire me..... I think I've told them a lot.....

But how can I tell them everything?..... I know. Father says He wants us to start thinking about positive things..... I know how bad the world is. We have to tell them what's waiting for them, He says. What to expect in the kingdom.....

(laughs) You know what I think. I think they need to see You coming out of the tabernacle once in awhile..... I guess You're right. To have them believe it constantly, You'd have to do it every day, like the apparitions. What makes us forget so easily, Butchie?..... I call it humanness, but that's a cop-out. The saints were human. What's the matter with us?..... **Even if we see and we believe for the**

moment, we forget tomorrow. What is the matter with us? Does original sin touch there? Why can't we grasp the truth and hang on to it?.....

If You stepped out of the tabernacle, say at Mass tomorrow morning, they'd be oohing and ahhing, and talking about it all day. And I'm sure people would come to the church...... **But then it would die down again.** What do we need to keep going in Your love? Maybe a booster shot would help..... I know. I hear that over and over again. **Faith.** We need some more teachings on faith.....

You know what I want to talk to You about? I want to talk to you about something really serious..... *(laughs)* Well, this time I want to be serious because I want to know, Butchie..... Butchie, stop it and listen to me..... I know, but You're not listening fully to me. Your fooling around. Listen to what I'm going to say. This is important stuff..... *(laughs)* Butchie, please listen to me, or I'll tell the Father..... Well, it's about priests seeking experiences. I want to know. I want to know what I don't know..... *(laughs)* Practically everything I don't know.....

How do you want us to enter into this prayer life?..... Seeking experiences or seeking You and waiting for them to happen?..... **A young girl and a boy.....** No. I don't believe they're going to seek an experience. They're seeking their lover, and to have their love returned..... No, I don't think they're going to seek an experience of sex. At least, not wholesome ones, Butchie..... Well, they're seeking love, love of each other..... **Falling deeper in love. Marriage. Children. But then, on the other hand** – what?..... **Some will seek an experience, then when it's over, there's nothing.** I don't know if I like that comparison too much. Give me something else..... I will think of it, but tell me something more.....

All right. **When they're going with each other, they fall deeper and deeper in love with each other, because they have knowledge of each other, of their likes and their dislikes..... But it's only through love that they find the experience of marriage.** And You mean a priest or anyone looking for an experience in the prayer life, should first fall in love with Jesus, and then the experiences will happen. And if they seek an experience, then they're going to come to a dead end..... Is it that much, **nine times out of ten?**.....

All right, give it to me once more..... *(laughs)* Don't do that. See, as soon as I stop, You've got to fool around again. I'm serious, Butchie. Tell me again now..... **A young couple find they like each other and they're attracted to each other. Then they fall deeper and deeper in love. But the experience of marriage comes through love.....** So say a priest wants a mystical union with the Father, or with you, Butchie, then they've got to work for Your love. Find out more about each other. Fall deeper in love with each other. And then, the jackpot is the experiences, right? But don't go in looking for the experiences, go in looking for a deeper knowledge of each other, and a deeper love.....

Yes, I'll buy that. Yes. I'm satisfied with that..... Thank You so much. I'm not very bright, and I can't understand all the things that are placed before me..... I know, Butchie, but my experiences are different. I've always known You, and I've always loved You..... That's right, I did love You as a brother, and I knew You as a brother, and I fell in love with You later as a lover because I loved everything You did as my friend and my brother. And that brought me into a deeper relationship which was a deeper love, and a new door opened..... **It's impossible to have an experience unless we're falling in love with You, because it's love that opens the doors to all these beautiful new awarenesses and experiences of You.....**

(laughs) You're forever opening doors..... I don't want You to open a door now. Stop changing the subject. I like the subject..... *(laughs)* **You don't like the subject but You like the person.** I'm talking real stuff now, and I have to know these answers, Butchie. I feel pretty dumb..... No..... Because You know that I melt, and I'm not giving You the chance to melt me, so keep talking.....

(laughs) He's looking at You like he understands..... **He does.....** Puppy, I love you so much. I'm so happy Butchie put you here in my valley, and it won't be long before I'm with you. And Butchie

loves you so much..... He does understand, doesn't he, Butchie? I hurt so much for you. I never got over the pain of losing you, Puppy, but now I think I have because I know you're here..... Look what he's doing, Butchie. He understands everything.....

I think this is the most beautiful spot ever. I don't think there's another spot as beautiful. If I were a painter, I would paint it..... No one would believe it. They wouldn't even know where I got the idea of painting it..... No. I don't think any brush could ever do it justice, Butchie. It wouldn't give the softness of the trees, the clearness of the brook. I don't think anybody could touch it, just the Father.....

No, Father. I knew You were close by. I could feel Your presence. I was telling Butchie this is such a beautiful spot. I think it's the most beautiful spot in the kingdom, and You've given it to me. Oh, I wish I were a painter or an artist, but I don't think anyone could understand its beauty..... *(laughs)* He was teaching me..... No, Father, I like to learn about these things. It was about experiences. I was asking Butchie. Is it right to look for experiences in prayer? I don't really know how to explain these things, my Father.....

I don't have to explain them. But I didn't know what to say about it when I was asked. But now I do. Not that I'm volunteering the information. But at least it sets my mind straight, Father..... I don't know. I think the greatest experience is falling in love with Jesus. Because only in loving Him, do I find You, Father. No experience could compare to this. This is the greatest one of all, and if it springs from love, Father, then we've got to get with falling in love, or else everything will be shallow and empty, and we'll forget.....

Yes, Father, it's like when I was rested in the Spirit in my bedroom that time. It was the love of Butchie and His beauty that brought that on. But it was because I loved him so much. It was a nice experience but it was because of love..... **Always in every experience, first is the love. There is no experience without love.** That would make a nice tape, right, Father?.....

I learn so much when I'm here, Father. I hate to go back. Not just for that reason. Because I love being here. I love the peace that I find here..... I will never be lonesome here, Father. How could I be lonesome with You and Butchie and Carsha?.....

It seems so far away from me..... The days seem longer. They seem harder for me. The nights are longer..... Do you notice when I wake up how I call for You, Father?..... I want You with me every minute, and I want to know You're there..... That's my greatest hurt, Father. But You know how much I hurt in different places. But it's nothing compared with being separated from You, Father..... Nobody will ever know how much I ache to be with You forever.....

That's my purgatory, being separated from You and Butchie and not being here in the valley. I don't think any purgatory could be worse. But that's Your fault too, Father. You gave me a taste of all of this. Then you send me back to my world, and then I hurt and I ache and I'm lonesome.....

I don't think they would ever understand how much I want to be here..... Well, I don't know about being special, but I hope You see the love that I hold for You, Father. I guess that makes me special. I don't know. It's Your doing Father, not mine.....

Gee, how I wish they could see You now, as I see You, Father. I can tell them but You know, Father, I think that they will not understand. Look at Father M, he says that nobody knows the Father except the Son and those He wishes to reveal Him to. But he thinks that's the end of it..... And many priests, like Father John, he says nobody sees God. Father, they don't know that I can see You, my Father, and there are veils between us. What's wrong with us, Father?..... But that's negative thinking..... If he walks around with that thought, it's negative. Why doesn't he fall deeper in love with You?.....

I don't know if it's our teachings, but I'm happy the way You brought me up, Father. They're missing a lot..... *(laughs)* If you say so. **I'll give them a little bit of Heaven through the revelations You have given me.** Carsha will lead me, right?..... They love it, Father. Don't You see the expressions on their faces? They love to know about Your kindness, Your love, Your beauty. They want to know about the valley and the trees and the brook and the angels. They want to know everything.....

Thomasino did..... I didn't tell anybody..... No. I made believe I forgot his feast day. That wasn't a lie. I just acted surprised, but I didn't tell anybody, Father. It was the most beautiful sight I have ever seen. The singing was just beautiful. I never knew anything could go so high. It was even higher than the highest cord on a violin. It was beautiful, Father..... But how can I tell them this?..... Of course I'll do anything You say. Everything You say is just super. If that's what You want, then that's what we'll do.....

I'm filled with love to overflowing..... I'm listening..... When You tell me, I can remember well, and it will come out at the right time, Father. Sometimes I think it's too much for me to handle, but it always comes out, and I know it's Carsha doing it at the right time..... **Then if we try to build up these priests and lead them into a deeper union and holiness with God, then those that are not so straight-laced will follow.....** I agree, Father. I think it's far better than chastising them..... You'll have to teach me Your gentleness, Father..... *(laughs)* You chastise me with so much love, it's almost like You're patting my hand.....

More than anything in the whole world, I love You. I love You so much, at times I feel like my heart is going to burst, and I almost hope that it does because then I will be with You.

EASTER. THE CHOIRS OF ANGELS

April 10, 1985

This is the first time I have flown in the valley, Butchie. We can see everything and it's more beautiful than ever. But where are we going? I feel like a kite..... You better hold me tight so I won't fall.

They're all so beautiful..... I know, choirs of angels. So beautiful. Each one is more beautiful than the other..... Coolra, Coolra. The angels praise and worship their God.

Why haven't You taken me here before, Butchie?..... There are different choirs. And Michael and Gabriel and Raphael are the closest to the Father's throne......

It's beautiful, Father. I've seen them when You come down to my valley and they come with You, but I've never seen so many..... Their songs are beautiful..... I have never heard such voices..... I can't pick them out, Father. Each voice is more beautiful than the other. You said they're spirits but you give them places. Father, there's so much in the kingdom I can't grasp. But I know you will give me the grace to understand this..... I thought my valley was the most beautiful place of all, but now I see there's so much more..... I can see why You never tire of it, Butchie. It's so beautiful. I don't think they would understand it. It brings to mind the Scripture.

I wish Butchie and I could stay here forever. I know I have to return..... No, I don't want to go back, but I know You want me to go back for now...... Father, who would want to go back after being here? I was wondering about it in the Scripture. The kingdom, if it were of this world, the soldiers would have behaved differently, they would have left Him alive.....

I'm looking. Butchie! Be serious. I don't want to miss anything..... I know, Butchie, but that was Your doing. I didn't walk away from You, You hid on me. So give me a chance to enjoy this or I'll go away on You. Tell Him, Father..... I want to see all of Michael's men..... There must be thousands and thousands..... Oh, they're so beautiful..... But they are giants, Father. I don't blame You for not wanting to walk the earth as a human. If I had all of this I wouldn't want the earth either..... **Only in spirit because You have to.** But I wouldn't go there either. It's more beautiful here, Father. And every time You show me something so beautiful, I don't want to go back.

How come You're showing me all this, Father?..... I know You love me, but You didn't show it to me before and You loved me before..... *(laughs)* Its filling me with so much love.....

I don't know, Father. I think I know what You want me to say, but I'm not quite sure if that's what I want to say. You want me to say the gift of resolution to cut free from the world. I would love it, but I don't know if I can do it. Especially by myself, I know I can't..... I thought that's why You put a box or a cage over me, and You cut me free from the world forever..... I think, Father, it will be difficult, because of my service, and how they flock to me after it.

You know I had a dream. I dreamt I fell asleep crying, "Father," because I missed You so much. And I dreamt You came and You kissed me and I felt Your kiss. It was warm and gentle and loving. But then I woke up. I felt peaceful. I wanted to *[believe it was You.]*..... Then it wasn't a dream, Father.

During Lent I know You love me, but I find it hard to grasp, my Father *[because then He and Jesus are not visibly present to her]*..... It's hard for me to understand it. I want to understand it..... I may have a small light on it now, but I wouldn't want to go through it again. Nope. Nope..... Yes, I love all of this. I love seeing them all, but I'd rather not go through it again right now, thank You..... Nope. I don't even want to talk about it, Father. I want to talk about something else, thank You..... I don't think I'm playing. I'm very serious, Father. You know my heart, I'm speaking truth. No way would I want to go through that again..... I believe You..... I know. I understand now, but I didn't understand it then, Father. It's easy to understand something when it's over, but I couldn't understand it when I was in the midst of it..... No, I know You love me, but I couldn't even say that then. Now I can say it. Father, You can do anything You want to me, but I would never want You to do that again..... Nope, I don't want to talk about it for another fifty years, never mind next year..... Nope.....

(laughs) You're not supposed to say "that bag of apples." That's my expression, Father. You're funny..... I believe You, Father. I love You so much. I love You even more. I'm kind of upset with You, but I do love You, and I never stopped loving You..... I know I tried. I really tried not to love You so much, because if I didn't love You so much, I wouldn't hurt so much, Father.

Look at Butchie. All He does is look at me silly. He looks like a silly billy. Butchie, I love You so much. And we love the Father so much, right? Wouldn't we like to stay here all the time with Him? *(laughs)* I'm trying to bribe Him. You know, Father, each time I hope it's this one.... Well, let's get it done fast then, Father, so I can come to You quickly.....

Father, it's a feast to my eyes, not just You, Father. But You are all beautiful..... I can't even say how much I love You, Father. It's seems like it's way down deep, but I know it's there. I'm just so filled with love for You, but I can't seem to get it all out..... That's the way I feel. It's just there and it keeps coming, and coming. And it seems like it goes down to a bottomless pit. And it expands and expands..... **The mystery of love is being unraveled. It's a gift to me. The mystery of love is beginning to unravel**. That is beautiful, Father. That is a beautiful gift. Father, I just love it.

And I love being here and seeing all the choirs of angels. It's the first time You allowed me to come here, Father..... Yes, they have come to the valley..... **I can't come by myself, only when Butchie takes me.....**

Everything's so beautiful, more than ever this Easter.... I didn't want anything to be given to me *[as an Easter present and to make up for the absence of the Father and Jesus during Lent]*. I just wanted You, and then that's everything. Just You, Father, to be in Your presence..... *(laughs)* And Yours too, Butchie, You silly. He always thinks He's getting left out. You are so silly, Butchie *(laughs)*.....

Butchie promised to take me here again. Father said, You have the key that opens the door to this plateau, and nobody can come .....

I'm glad to be home. I never want to be away from You again. You're everything to me, Father, and I can't take it when You're gone. You've ruined me rotten, and I can't take it when You leave me, so I shift the blame to You again..... Yes, I did. I envied those who had never seen You. Because they weren't hurting. I really envied them, Father..... If You want me to. We'll both put our arms around You, Father. Carsha's standing in here too. We're a wonderful circle of love. Oh Father, this is where I belong forever. Please don't go away from me again.

EILEEN DELIGHTS IN THE HELP OF THOMAS AND CATHERINE

April 21, 1985

I don't have to call you. You know that I love you..... You do? Well I'm all ears and I want to listen. And if Butchie finds it appropriate that you come, then it must be very special..... I can't imagine, Thomasino..... My mission? Well, to make the Father known, to bring Carsha in a new light as a person..... Yes, Thomasino, I was telling Butchie this over and over again. I feel like I'm going to be blocked in many directions..... Yes, it's true. **Those that really want to be better will profit.....**

What about you, Thomasino?..... When you brought the doctors new lights were you rejected?..... *(laughs)* It sounds funny to hear you speak like that: "left field." No, I won't budge.....

But Thomasino you were a scholar, I'm a nothing. I depend totally and completely on Carsha. If Carsha gives me the light, then I can say it, but I can't dig into books like you do..... Well, because you're always quoting to me, that's why..... See, you're doing it now. I don't understand this stuff..... Well, if it's coming from Carsha it has to be truth..... That's right..... And I can't back down.....

You really think so?..... Yes, that's what the Father has been saying, right, Butchie? **It's not by prayer alone that this ministry will flourish, it's by penance, by suffering.** I understand that..... But what is it you wanted to say, Thomasino?..... Me? *(laughs)* That's a laugh. I can't even write a letter. I hate doing it because I have to look up the words in the dictionary..... *(laughs)* That would be a miracle in itself. Me. *(laughs)* You're foolish sometimes.....

But you were intelligent, you're one of the greatest doctors of the Church. I'm a nothing, Thomasino, and I'm fully aware of it. And I'm very comfortable with it..... Nope, I'm not trying to increase my knowledge, except knowledge from the Holy Spirit, and I'm not studying to catch up. I don't feel like it..... I remember that. You said you got more from the tabernacle than from books...... Yes, in my quiet moments with Butchie.....

Really? Is that why you're here?..... You know, Thomasino, sometimes I get very frightened..... No. No, I don't doubt Him at all. How could I doubt Carsha? Of course not. I get frightened of myself because I know I'm dumb and I'm stupid, and that's certainly not false humility. I know what I am. I always get so deathly ill at the beginning of a service..... I just wonder what they expect from me. What can I give them, through grace. And in my humanness I get scared..... *(laughs)* Why would you be glad of that? *(laughs)* That's for sure, I'd never be overconfident. I trust. I can't do this of myself. I depend on Carsha, for sure.....

Oh, sure I will. Any place the Father wants me to go, I will go. But what's your real reason for being here, Thomasino?..... I'm listening to you..... It's going to get a little difficult for me then. All right..... **I must never waver in doctrine or tradition.....**

(laughs) I'm not that serious. It's you that's doing it. If you want me to laugh, I will laugh – whenever you make a face..... I'm really listening to you, Thomasino, because I want to do everything you want me to do. **All right, I will never waver by grace in doctrine or tradition. And whenever I see the light of the Holy Spirit, I will not back down.** But isn't that pride?..... Not when it's coming from Carsha..... For sure I know what I'm capable of doing..... **I must shine as a beacon of light for all in the darkness that has fallen upon the Church.** My Father said that once..... **There are going to be winds, and there are going to be storms..... A tree, the leaves fall. The tree has its roots deep into the earth. So my roots will be deeply in my Father's love..... I'll be batted to the left and to the right, but I will bounce back and stand tall and firm on my Father's words. And when I pass from this world, they will know that I stand on truth.....**

(laughs) A lot of good it will do then. What are they going to do to me now?..... Yes *(laughs)*, I am afraid. Of course I'm scared. Weren't you ever afraid?..... *(laughs)* You are silly. You are funny. I know you stood firm on doctrine and tradition. And I need grace. And I need help. And I need your intercession.....

Bishops?..... **Bow on their knees in humility.** What do you mean by that? They'll clobber me if they don't agree with me..... **Then they'll really know that this is the truth that they should be doing.** I want to keep peace with them, Thomasino..... **The only way I can keep peace with them is to speak the truth in sound doctrine and tradition. This will bring them to their senses and to their knees in all humility.....**

Kind of frightening..... I know you don't mean to frighten me..... What about them? They're liberal, they won't like it..... Liberal? I don't know, being free, pulling doctrine and tradition in all directions..... **Then if they fight against me, that means they know it's truth......** That's one way of looking at it.

(laughs) Nope. No. I appreciate all you do for me, Thomasino, and I'm so glad you were at my last service. Will you be at this one with me? I need your strength. The crowds are getting bigger, and I see Butchie walking amongst them, but I feel so good knowing you're there.....

I know, my Father told me why I must suffer, Catherine, because prayer isn't enough for the services. The Father wants them to flourish, and to touch many souls because this is a real serious hour for the Church.....

I mind. Sure I mind, because I don't like to suffer, Catherine. But now I find it easier..... No. I try not to mention that any more now that I know. **Silent suffering is one of the greatest prayers that I can give for this ministry next to Butchie and the Eucharist.....** I think that's wonderful. How about you, Thomasino? Do you think that's great?..... *(laughs)* Yeah, he laughs..... *(laughs)* You're funny. I'm not used to your talk, for sure..... I appreciate you both standing so close to me and Butchie and Carsha and my Father..... The Father has called me to this mission, Thomasino, and I delight in your help.....

Yes, I saw all of the angels. An abode of the Father in the kingdom, where He rests..... I couldn't tell you how many, Thomasino. I know how much you love them. But there were so many. Ever so many..... I can, through Carsha. I have to be so careful, Thomasino. Surely, you must know the rejection when you bring in something new, but I want to stand firm on doctrine and tradition. I remember everything you told me, right, Butch?..... Yes. *(laughs)* He says right..... Yes, it's growing. I'm sure that's the reason He let you come to me. It is growing. And more people are hearing about it, and getting interested in it. So I can understand your concern, Thomas, but I won't waver, by grace and acceptance to grace.....

(laughs) The Big Guy? *(laughs)*..... Father, Butchie brought Thomasino and Catherine to me. He said he has things to teach me and he said I need it now more than ever because the ministry is growing..... Many things, Father. That I must stand straighter than ever on the doctrine and tradition of the Church, and that I must never waver no matter, even if they come at me ready to pierce my very heart and soul. I must not waver. He said he was going to help me with many of these priests, Father. That many more want to come, and they're inquiring about the ministry. He said there was going to be a big change in the Church, and that I would shine like a beacon of light, Father, in the darkness that's overshadowing the Church at this moment.....

Oh no, You know how?..... Oh no, not that way. I feel like a black jelly bean in a bag of white jelly beans, Father..... Yes, like an oddball. They're so knowledgeable about everything, and I don't know too much. Catherine said that my suffering is to help the ministry, because not by prayer alone will it survive, but by suffering, as Jesus has suffered..... Oh sure I agree, Father. I know how much You love me, and You don't want me to suffer needlessly, but I remember what You said about Lent. "I love you so much, Eileen, and I wanted so much to run to you, but I knew in this suffering, this emptiness, you were drawing closer to Me and the kingdom, so I did what was right."

I'll never forget that, Father, You wanted to come to me. But the most important thing was the spiritual growth of my soul, not the comforting of my body that houses my soul. So I keep running back to that, Father, and every time I do I grasp it in a fuller way..... Because You teach me.....

(laughs) You know what he said? He said they *[a group of her heavenly friends]* would all sit up in the balcony *[of St. John's church]* and I would see them. *(laughs)* That would be something..... No. I know they love me and I love them. I know Thomasino is going to instruct me, Father..... No. I'm delighted that Butchie did this for me..... He did? *(laughs)* I knew He would never do it without asking You, Father.....

I think we're on the brink of something great. Great for You, my Father, to bring You all the glory that You deserve. To bring You ever so many souls. I just feel so happy to be a part of it, even if I feel like a black jelly bean among the white ones..... I would suffer anything and go any place and do anything to bring You the joy that You so rightfully deserve, Father.....

I like being a beacon of light in the dark times of the Church. I like even more being the beacon of light that lights up Your face, my Father. To have You look at me so lovingly. It thrills me to death. That's the most important thing in my life.

LAUGHTER IS FREEDOM OF EXPRESSION

May 5, 1985

Yes I know that song well. It's one of my favorites, Butchie. But I never heard You sing it before. It means so much more to me now..... *(laughs)* Nobody pictures You singing, but I know You sing and You laugh. And you laugh and you play and you cry. I guess we kind of figure you to be a little bit starchy..... That's right. **What is life without laughter. Laughter is freedom. Freedom of expression.**

Sing it to me again..... I know, but I like to hear You sing it because You never sang it before. I'd like to hear you sing it again..... That's the part I like the best.....

I like everything about You. What do You mean the best? *(laughs)* There's no best about You. I like everything..... *(laughs)* I am thinking..... Probably when You hold me. I feel safe, secure, loved..... You're being silly. How do I know?.... I guess when You look at me, I feel like I'm the only one that matters..... Oh, there are so many things, Butchie. Don't try to pin me down to one thing..... No, there is nothing I dislike. I love everything about You..... The way You hold my hand, pat my head. The way you look at me. Your concern for me. The way You love me. I could go on and on, Butchie.

You're just so good..... *(laughs)* I was thinking about that..... It's more than space. It's not like my sky..... I like to see the clouds racing by. Like when we were kids, remember? We'd make all kinds of figures out of them. I like that.....

I remember that. I remember how You laughed..... Because I never considered You the Father's Son. I remember that discussion well..... You asked me where Heaven was and I said, "Butchie, I don't really know, but I'll tell you a secret. I think it's in a valley. A hidden valley that no explorers have discovered." And You laughed so much, I'll never forget it. Even then You had secrets..... I never dreamed it was so beautiful. But You let me rave on and on..... I don't remember all of that. Did I really say that?..... **I did.** "I think I'll take You with me there forever." *(laughs)* See, even then I loved You..... Well, maybe not this way, but I loved You and I wanted You to be with me. We had such fun.....

You like to put me in this mood of reminiscing, don't you? *(laughs)*..... No, I'm never afraid of that. You're not afraid of that, are You, Butchie?..... No way. The more I love You, the more I depend upon You..... I guess we have come a long way..... No. I loved the fun we had when we were kids. But I love our relationship better now..... I was thinking about it in bed last night. All the things You did for me, and I was so dumb and stupid and I couldn't grasp it. I didn't try. Like when You kissed my cut and it healed. And the *[ragged edged]* glass, it never cut me.....

I remember that. We were looking for Indian arrows, and I was stuck in that cave, and You let the wild rocks fall away from me. All You did was touch the rocks, and they fell apart so I could climb out..... **You left them that way.** *(laughs)*..... That cave has been there for years and years..... Yes, we have so many secrets..... No, nobody would understand them.....

I don't know if I know how much, but I know You do..... I really know You do. But I don't think I can quite grasp how much..... I would just love to stay and talk all day with You. Each time I leave You, it gets harder and harder..... What's so good about that?....

I don't even want to talk about that because it seems like You're always promising. I'm not used to Your time, nor my Father's. And it seems like it's going to be forever. So I don't want to talk about it now, I just want to enjoy it *[here]*..... I get angry when I think about it *[about others dying before her]*..... I don't know. They would think I was a dopey one. But they don't understand how much I love You and I want to be with You..... I'll go along with that. But how many years do I have to be purified? It seems like forever.....

Well, somebody else will come and touch them and save them. Father always has somebody else..... **But for now He wants me, but it won't be forever.....**

(laughs) You're beautiful..... I wish everyone could see You like this, Butchie. You can laugh and laugh and play. We only know

You, Butchie, as the starchy Son. They don't know how much You laugh..... You see, I have an edge on them, Butchie. That's why I love You so much. I have an edge on these people and it's not their fault. The Father has chosen me. I'm glad of that..... Thank You so much. I love You too.....

I don't know. Love means something different here. The moment I say it I can feel a tingling in my feet, in my brain, in my fingertips. It means all, totally and completely all..... It's not just a word here..... I feel so much love from You, it's almost like a magnet filling my very soul. But then I get nervous, I wonder what You're up to. There's something around the corner, Butchie..... Yes, You do. But when it's so overflowing, You've got something up Your sleeve..... *(laughs)* You know what I mean. I've got to watch it..... You're funny..... Is that what You call it? *(laughs)* I mean You're so loving and extra loving and when You look at me like that You've got something that's cooking. Or You know something's ahead.....*(laughs)* The Father's been giving it to me since Lent. You better knock it off because You haven't prepared me.....

I don't know. I think my salvation. I know my salvation, that's what You've prepared me for. When You put it like that, who can lose?....I know that. **To fall in love with You with deeper love, then I'll function better in the ministry to the Father's people. And I will draw them as a magnet to my Father**..... You don't have to do all these things to make me fall deeper in love with You. I didn't think it could be possible. Yet, knowing You, everything's possible.....

Yes, Father. *(laughs)* I'm just wondering why Butchie's so extra loving and attentive today. When He does it this much, I get nervous..... Oh no, Father. Nor would I ever refuse. Butchie said the deeper I fall in love with Him, the more it will reflect to Your children, and I will draw them as a magnet to Your heart, my Father.....

What's that, Father?..... **There is a great work for me, and I shall have time to accomplish it..... I must spend more time in silence and solitude.** You've told me this before..... **But this time it's an act of obedience to my Father. Every word that I say will be weighed**

by the Holy Spirit, and every word will be a priceless gem given to each person, each child of the Father. It must be placed gently upon the soul, and they must treasure it and change and become better people. This cannot be done unless I radiate my love for Jesus, my Father, and the divine Holy Spirit..... My time is short. My Father, I'm delighted, and I want to accomplish everything You want me to accomplish in this time..... **I will not take my commitments lightly. I will pray to Carsha for enlightenment, and I will be united to Jesus in the Eucharist. And I will isolate myself from all. This will be my preparation for my services. And then the jewels will flow to each and every one of them, and they will hunger and they will thirst for their God.....** Father, I do want them to follow Your word.....

They do. They truly know that I radiate Your love..... I'm at peace, Father. I'm listening closely..... **A stream of grace, a real explosion of love for the Father.** I'm just happy to be that instrument, Father..... My diocese? I don't know. I don't really know, Father..... I do believe You, because You know all things.....

You said I would ride a white charger of faith..... I remember that..... I will, my Father, I'll remember that. **There's so much to do, and such a short time. My time is truly running low, like a candle.** But that candle is less now, Father..... And that's as much time as I have.....

No, I'm not afraid, are You kidding? I'm delighted. I wish Carsha would blow a breeze on it so the candle would burn faster..... **But He will. He will blow the power and wisdom and light of the Father on this ministry.....** I still have my eyes on that candle.

Oh Father, I am so happy about it..... I am just so happy. I kept wondering if You were forgetting me. Were You going to leave me here forever..... No, I'm happy to see that candle's less than half.....

Yes, Father. I wanted to ask You about that, and I kept forgetting. **Then it's not in a proper spirit. They're always looking for new things, but it's in the true doctrine and tradition of the Church that they will find a new awakening: the burst of light, of wisdom,**

and of knowledge, and their identity and truth..... No. I'm glad you settled that in my mind. I kept forgetting to ask You, Father, if this was right or wrong.....

I believe You, Father, and I'll remember that..... I will repeat it, Father. **I must stay in recollection and prayer within my own household and prepare myself for all the commitments that my Father places before me. Stay always in the love of my Savior, my spouse Jesus. Stay close to Him in the Eucharist. Cut free. It is now the hour for Him. And Carsha will give me the light. There will be a terrific explosion of faith in God's people.....**

I'll remember, Father. And You'll remember the candle *(laughs)*..... I love You so much, Father. I always complain about Your time because I want to be with You forever..... I know, Father, and I'm blessed, but I know there's much more love here and I want to be part of it. I can't have it unless I'm here forever. So I'm selfish, I guess..... Because You love me..... Yes, I know what to do. I know what to do, Father.....

You touch my face and brush my hair. Your love is in every touch. It sinks deep into my soul, my Father..... You do this to me and for me, and then You wonder why I can't be without You.

MOTHER'S DAY

May 12, 1985

My eyes are just feasting on the beauty, Butchie. I just feel so much welling up inside of me. I just can't express my emotions...... I really don't know. It's a place where we can communicate, a place where we can love and we can talk and we can laugh. A place where there's peace and tranquility, and nothing bothers me..... No, I've been down this path how many times, and each time there's more beauty, different beauty..... Well it seems as though You're trying to reveal so much to me.....

I don't know. **What does it mean to be a bride of Christ?**..... I know, but I didn't know then. You were my friend, remember?..... *(laughs)* It tickles me. Now I know You were from an early age, but I didn't know it then. I know it now *[when Eileen was two or three, Jesus, appearing as a child a couple of years older, became her companion, telling her, "Call me* Butchie, *and I'll call you* Slug.*" In these first years of their friendship, she did not know her friend Butchie was Jesus, nor did she know as a teenager that He was leading her to a spiritual betrothal and marriage]*..... Well I think I would have shied against it *[had I known]*..... I really don't know, Butchie..... *(laughs)* I know You just don't pick them out of the sky. I know You have a plan with the Father and Carsha..... I don't know if I got into it that deep..... *(laughs)*

See, I'm just a human person, living in the world, I can't understand all this love. I do and I don't..... *(laughs)* See there You go again. I really don't know..... *(laughs)* I understand Your love, and I understand Carsha's love to a certain point, and I certainly delight in and understand my Father's love..... I know there's no jealousy in the love. And yet, I don't act the part, because I keep asking You to come with me to the Father, because I don't want You to feel slighted. And I keep calling and making sure Carsha's there.

You see, my humanness goes back to my worldliness, I guess. I know without a doubt there's no jealousy in the three Persons, just deep, deep love. Then my humanness takes over. I guess that's what You mean, isn't it?..... *(laughs)* You just have to give me the light to see it. I love You all so much, so very much, but each in a different way..... Well, it's hard to explain. But see then that humanness comes in. I want You to all know that I love You all so much, and I don't want You to feel left out, and I know You're not left out, but that's where the humanness comes in..... *(laughs)* You are cuckoo..... *(coughs)* I hope You don't catch my germs..... *(laughs)* **You can't.** Invisible shield..... No. Maybe I'm allergic to You. That would be funny, huh?..... No way.....

I don't want to do that. I want to talk about business. I want to talk about stuff, lots of stuff..... *(laughs)* Lots of things. Maybe not more important, but I want to talk about things..... I want to talk about Your love, Carsha's love, and the Father's love..... I want to know more about Carsha. I know You want me to know more about Carsha. I want to know about this great love that springs from the Father and the Son. I want to know so much about it, Butchie, that I hurt inside.....

(laughs) No. Butchie, there is so much to this world. How can I explain it. They'll think I'm a dodo bird..... Oh, I hunger and thirst because they don't see as I see, Butchie..... How can I be their eyes?..... I do that at times. They can understand a little bit about the kingdom..... I get nervous before my service, but then Carsha takes over. I get nervous before the theologians. They're so bright, and I'm not bright at all..... Yes, but that's infused wisdom. They studied theirs..... There's so much I want to know about You. Each time I see You, You're more beautiful.

It blows my mind all the patience You had with me growing up, Butchie, as my friend, my brother, my spouse. I couldn't have had that patience with anybody. You had so much patience with me..... Even now, I know what should be done, and I just don't seem to have the strength to do it. I try hard, Butchie. You're there with me. You see how hard I try..... I know it did. It penetrated my very soul. I don't know how to even express that. It touched the depths of something inside of me, not touching the shell of the body, but something touched the depths inside of me..... **That's my soul. And that something is Carsha, His love.....**

I wouldn't know how to explain this..... **It's like the body being a robot, and the soul inside** *[it is]* **the invisible motor that makes it function. Take the motor out of the robot, or the soul out of me, and there's nothing.** Then, the soul is very important, not only for this life, but for the next..... **More so.** More so..... I can't fully understand that, Butchie.

You had me see Thomasino, and You had me see Catherine *[of Siena]*. Of course I believe my Father can do all things, but sometimes I wonder, why this mystery? Why aren't their bodies in the grave? Why do You allow me to see them as they looked?..... Yes, the Father can do all things..... **So I can identify them.** That's important. Right now, it's important. See, I was confused about it..... For sure I do believe that the Father can do anything, and if He finds fit for me to see Thomasino the way he looked, and Doctor Mellifluous *[St. Bernard of Clairvaux]*, Catherine, and Martin *[de Porres]*, and all the rest, that's His will, and it's OK. And they'll even be more beautiful in their risen bodies, for sure.....

(laughs) I probably won't even know them. I'm glad, Butchie, because I was really confused. I accepted it, because that's the way the Father made me. But I often wondered, and I'm sure my Father knew I was wondering..... **God, my Father, can do all things. Accept His blessings and do not question them.** And that's what I do, I guess..... No, I wouldn't know Catherine then. How would I know her?..... Nope. There are many mysteries unfolding before me. Butchie, You're just so filled with mystery..... No, I delight in it, because there is never a dull moment in my life..... *(laughs)* Do I really give You that much trouble?..... Butchie, I love You so much. I just love You so much.....

Yes, there is love there for You, Father, a different love as my Daddy, but I love You too, my Father..... We were talking about many things, Father. The mystery of seeing Thomasino and Catherine, Doctor Mellifluous and Martin, and all the others. I'm sure You know at times I was so confused, but now I understand. I guess I've always understood Your greatness, Father..... No. I thank You for them all, for sure.....

Butchie said there was such a plan, even since He came to me when I was little. The perfect plan of the Father..... Yes, Father, I know there is..... **Because I will speak with determination. They will know that I know my Father, and I know Butchie and Carsha. They'll know that I've been in the kingdom, and I've seen with my eyes what I speak of.....** Is that part of Your plan, Father?..... Then You do have work ahead for me?..... Really? I don't know. I have my eyes on the candle, not the ministry. The ministry will be all work, Father, and I'll do whatever You want. But my eyes are really on that candle, and I'm watching it closely..... *(laughs)* Did He really say that?..... **It would go right down to the bottom in a second** *(laughs)*.....

It's going to be a very important year in my life. If you say so, Father..... **It's going to be a very important year in the Church.** And I'll be part of it, my Father?..... If You say so..... You're kidding *(laughs)*..... No. I don't know, but it's not hard for me to believe, for who could be greater than You, Father?..... Because You say it, I believe it. Sure, Father. Sure I do..... I get impressed, my Father, but nothing impresses me as much as You do. Who's greater than You, Father. Not the President, nor the Pope..... I'd probably say "Oh," but You're the greatest, so they don't phase me, Father, and I thank You for this. I thank You so much..... And You're my life..... Well they're secondary, Father. To know and to love You is the greatest thing in my life.....

Oh sure, I was very impressed, and it's good..... No, I just wanted to impress You, Father, to do Your will, and if that's the way You want it, OK..... What two things?..... **It's going to be a powerful year in my life. This preaching ministry is going to be powerful and bring souls to You, my Father..... In droves.** That's good..... Coming up the street? I don't remember. Oh, I remember. There were thousands, a million dandelion flowers in the field. And I said, "My Father, for every dandelion flower I see, I want to save a million souls. You're God and You can do anything. Take this pledge from me, Father." And you did? You don't miss a trick, Father..... Boy, then You're going to have a lot of souls, because there are a lot of dandelion flowers *(laughs)*..... **I must make your children God centered because I am God centered.** I guess so, Father. Sometimes I don't feel so God centered, I feel self-centered.

Look what I did with poor Jude, you'll never find him down there..... Well, I don't know if he's chuckling or not, I'll take Your word for it. But I'm really mad at him, Father..... He does delight in it? Well he won't delight so much when I don't even say a word to him again..... Nope. I never prayed to him before, and I'll never pray to him again, and You better tell him...... Well, that will be up to him, Father. A promise is a promise, and that's what I promised, and that's what he got..... No. Do You know how many people I told to pray to him? At least fifteen or twenty. And now I'm not telling any more, because he doesn't stand on his word..... That's my judgment. Father, I have to see, to feel, to touch, to understand, and I don't understand where he's coming from, and I don't understand about him, and if he wants to make it right with me, he better answer my prayer. And it's not a selfish plea, Father. Not for me, for sure.....

(laughs) I plead my case, and that's it, right? All right. We'll leave it there..... *(laughs)* That's silly..... No..... Nope. *(laughs)* How can Butchie say that? I don't have any statues of You, Father. I won't put You there. No..... No, not even if I had a statue, which I don't..... Yes, I've turned Butchie around a couple of times. Put a bag on His head..... Once I did, and then He yelled. *(laughs)* If anyone ever heard Him, they'd think the house was haunted. He was just being silly, my Father.....

Mary? For sure..... My Mother. It's a privilege to see you, Mother, and I'm glad it's Mother's Day..... Did you really like it? I wish I could have done so much more..... I love you so much, and many times my love for you is misunderstood, but you know how much I love you.....

It's Mother's Day, and you gave me the biggest present of all. I'm so happy you're pleased with it..... If I'm around next year, I'll make one even more beautiful..... It's enough knowing that you know that I love you..... Are you really pleased with me as a bride to your Son even when I fall and make so many bumps and bruises?..... Do you really like that? I mean considering all the struggle I had with the rosary?..... I'm happy you liked that..... For real?..... **You wait for me to say my rosary each day.** That's really beautiful..... The way a mother should. And you surely are my mother. I thank the Father for having you come to me today..... Did you like that? *(laughs)* My terrible voice..... I guess you don't miss too much..... Thank you so much, and I do love you. You know how much I love you, and I'm proud to be your daughter, ever so proud.

SOMETHING TO HOPE FOR

1985 (Otherwise undated)

I can't do the valley justice. I want to describe the trees to my people. I tell them of all these fruits, but I can't tell them what they are, Butchie.....

They are in awe over what I say, yes. But I wish I could go into more detail. I wish I could tell them that we can travel faster than time. I tell them it's always now. They look in awe and they are stunned..... But how can I tell them everything? They are so hungry for the knowledge of the kingdom. How can I tell them that we hold hands when we walk through this valley? Oh, we laugh and we laugh, we love, but how can I tell them this..... Yes, even walking in the water, and speaking with the fishes, Butchie. They are so hungry, and I feel so selfish because I can't put it across, as much as I want to.....

Yes, I know I whet their appetites..... Yes, they are beautiful. But how can I explain that time is always now, and that You gave me those baby birds in the nest, and that they will be mine forever in this stage *[always babies]*. They won't understand it..... I told them that there's no dying. The grass is crushed when you lie in it, and when you get up, it bounces right back.

Each time I come there's more beauty, and You're more beautiful, more gentle and more loving. I do want them to love You ever so much, but I want to love You the best. I want them to hunger and thirst after the kingdom.....

I agree with that. **They want to hear of everything positive. They need something to hope for, to look forward to.** But if they could only grasp it. If I could bring a picture back with me and show it to them..... But how can I paint it in their mind?..... **A love that lasts forever, until they come here**..... Yes, yes, I want them to understand there's so much more......I don't know how to work my way through it. I hope when I go this week to them I can. I'm sure Carsha will be there. I want them to look beyond the things of this world to a deeper, richer, fuller life.....

I find myself being shackled down..... Yes, I can feel Carsha helping me. I can almost scream when that phone rings..... We can't be of two worlds. We can live and function in this world, but we must live for the next. There's so much more, Butchie, how can I get it through to them? If You would take them all here for one day, I would have my problem and Yours solved. They would see.....

I ache for the Father. I want them to know what I know. I want them to see what I see, and hear what I hear, so they won't be shackled down..... I know. I saw their faces, and the silence was deeper than silence. Your silence overcomes their silence. Only You reveal the secrets of the kingdom..... We'll get through.....

No, I don't think so. You did it, I didn't do it...... I don't think it's modesty, I think it's truth, Butchie. Don't put any frosting on the cake. I know what I'm capable of doing. I love You for it, but I know me, and You know me...... You're so beautiful, so beautiful, and You know what the best part is, You never die. You'll be here for me when I come.

When are You going to take me to that plateau again so I can see the angels...... Really? No, I appreciate it, I know no one has ever been there. But You spoil me. Then when I want to go back again, You tell me it's a rare privilege. So You're to blame..... *(laughs)* I know. I wish I could describe it to them. Would they believe me, would they understand?

Butchie, they are so hungry for You, without even realizing it. They want to know more and more about You and the Father and about Carsha..... Yes, He's filling the church. I get afraid sometimes. I know it's Carsha who gives me the words, but in my humanness I say, what if I forget what to say, or run out of words..... No, I don't underestimate Him. I think it's my humanness taking over, Butchie. Many times I think You forget I'm a human..... *(laughs)* Maybe You forget You're the Son of the Father?.....

Don't do that, that hurts, you know..... You're funny. You'll have me like Pinocchio, pulling that nose forever, or squeezing my neck..... (laughs) Nope, now that I have seen it, I want to see it again and again and again. So now You have spoiled me. If You didn't want me to ask You shouldn't have shown me in the first place.....

There's always something beyond..... Butchie, You take me there and You show me different things I didn't see before. Yet they were always there..... Veils have slipped away. There are always veils slipping away revealing more beauty here in the valley. There were so many veils that I couldn't see it..... Isn't it growth? *(laughs)*..... **Spiritual growth.** I understand it now, but will they ever understand it?

The Father made our world so beautiful. One would never dream anything could be more beautiful, and yet look! Nothing could ever surpass this world. And I know there's much more to see. Especially here in the valley. Every time I come there's a different beauty. I hope I'll never go backwards, I wouldn't want to lose anything.....

No, I just love walking with You. It's so beautiful and so peaceful..... I told them about that. Even the trees acknowledge the Savior. And look at how the flowers and the fishes nod. But they have to see it to understand. It's a whole new world.

I have never seen such beauty. It's like all seasons in one. None interfering with the other, but always so present. It feels like I can just go from here to there, to enjoy my seasons, and yet, they are always present. It blows my mind today, Butchie. You've never shown me so much here. And yet, there's more to come.

How many veils are between me and my valley?..... You dare not say..... It would?..... *(laughs)* Do You see that splendor in my face because of the beauty I see?..... And it seems as though Your face changes with all the beauty and becomes even more beautiful than ever. At times I feel like it's impossible that You could be more beautiful. And yet with the increasing splendor of the valley Your splendor is increasingly beautiful..... Then the veils between us fall, right? Such a mystery to me. I know You don't mean it to be, but it is a mystery to me. It's so beautiful..... Oh, I want ever so much to come forever..... I remember the candle. *[When it burns to the bottom, Eileen will go to the valley]*. That hasn't passed from my thoughts at all..... Oh, what did I do to deserve all this? It's so beautiful today, the most it's ever been..... **You've always loved me.....** That's really beautiful. That's really poetic......

(laughs) I don't know. I can't measure it, Butchie. I don't know how to measure my love for You. You silly, silly..... I see. Your words come from the depths of something within me, and it just seems to swell, and swell to overflowing.....

I seem to understand that I'll be here soon. And it fills me with so much joy..... Probably, but I can't wait. But I know I must. I'll do everything the Father tells me to do.....

It's a promise, Father? For the first time I'm beginning to understand, it's not too far away. I know I stamp my feet and get angry, my Father, because I feel like I'm being cheated *[when others die before her]*. But I also know that You have something for me to do, and I want to accomplish it. I felt it in my last service. I felt it when I told them my only sorrow *[at my death]* would be that my time for merit would be over.

And then I want to stay around awhile and receive more merit, and do more things for You, Father. And I know that was You working within my soul. Here I am today, dying to get here, maybe a little impatient, and yet I know I have work to do...... I guess so, Father. Call it what You may, but that's a dreadful thought, that my time for merit will be over. It will be final. I won't be able to do anything more..... Then I feel as though I haven't accomplished enough, and I want to stay and do more.....

Oh, that was Butchie, He twisted the words. You know how silly He gets at times..... *(laughs)* Did You hear Him? He's really a silly kid, right? .....*(laughs)* But I love Him, Father..... Father, the valley is so beautiful today, it's more beautiful than its ever been and there's so much more to see.

You see, my Father, I realized the time here is always now, always present and never past, and never tomorrow, always present.

But I keep wondering how come I see new things that I didn't see before? I couldn't connect it with the time *[being always present]*, Father. Nor did I connect it with veils slipping away *[from the valley]*..... Father, I always connected veils slipping away with Your face becoming more beautiful, and my Butchie's, and Carsha's, because now I can see Him as a person, a person that I love so much. But I never connected veils with the valley, my Father.

The lighting is different. Everything is different. It's like kissed with a glow, not gold and not silver. A glow, like in the morning when the sun kisses the flowers. They come to life. Something is kissing them. I see the valley in a new and different way today.....

Oh, I know that, Father. They always say, you give the Father a finger, He gives you a hand. You're reversing it now. **"I give you so much, Child, but I'm going to ask you for much"**..... Well, I guess it does, a little, but I know You're there..... No, I won't be afraid. I love to have You talk like this to me. I understand You. You are going to ask much from me. And that's all right..... I like You to say it to me, Father. I think it gives me more confidence in You, Father.....

I promise I will, and Carsha will be ever so close to me..... No one, Father? **You mean no one has ever experienced Carsha like I have experienced Him?** I don't know if I could take more, Father. But there was a time that I believed He was power. Until You gave me the light to see Carsha, and Carsha revealed Himself to me as a person..... I don't know what I thought of Him, except as power and gifts..... I don't know, I've never seen His hands. I didn't know how the gifts came to me, except through power.....

(laughs) I don't know if I could stand more awakenings about Carsha..... I delight in His wisdom. I delight in what He does with me in my talks, because I know what I am capable of doing, my Father. And I thank You for making me aware of it, Father.....

Carsha, You're so important in my life. I thank You for coming to me today..... I love You so much. I know I couldn't function for my Father and for Butchie without You. I know I'm not bright, Carsha, but I know You give me the wisdom to do my Father's work.

I truly love You so much. I love You so much. And I need You so badly. I know we have a wedlock, and I delight in it and my Butchie and my Father delight in it. It's hard for me to grasp it, but I know You're there. I know that You do not let anyone fool me, nor do You intend to let them hurt me..... I do see the protection of light around me, and You do protect me as a spouse. I can't fully understand it, Carsha, but I know You give me the wisdom to see it. I feel it penetrating my very soul. I feel Your love in every part of my being..... I know I belong to You in a very special way, and I thank my Father, and I thank my Butchie. I want You to fill me with this love to overflowing.

But please, Carsha, there's something I'm going to ask You. Give me the wisdom and the strength to cut free from all men, to do my Father's will, Carsha. I can't function properly with all these people around me. Please, Love, help me to do my service to the best of my ability to please my Father. Please, Carsha, because we were joined in holy wedlock, separate me from the world. Please help me because I'm weak and I need Your strength. My Father wants this, Butchie wants this and I want it, Carsha. Please.

PART FOUR: REVEALING HEAVEN

ON THE BRINK OF A NEW AWAKENING

June 22, 1985

No, I just love being here, Butchie. When I'm home I don't get to the valley as often as I'd like to. But when I was in Philadelphia I had more time to withdraw at night in the quietness of my room, and I did delight in it. I miss the valley so much when I'm not here, Butchie. Each time I return it's more beautiful than ever. You're beautiful. And each bouquet You give me is more beautiful.....

I really don't know what to think about it. I felt like the running water at times. Running on and on and on, not looking back where I'm coming from, but always looking ahead just to see where I'm going. Other times I feel like the running deer, traveling swiftly through the valley, to reach higher places..... No. I would be stagnant then, and I don't ever want to be stagnant.....

You once told me the stream would run on and on, until it reaches the big lake and would be totally lost and consumed in the big lake, which is You, Butchie. That's how I feel right now..... No. I see my Father's hand upon me. No, I can truthfully say, Butchie – You know the secrets of my heart – it doesn't bother me. It doesn't swell my head or my mind. I'm just so glad it's over, and that Carsha came through to help me. There's no room for pride there, Butchie, You know that. And that's a grace from the Father.....

Surely it's a grace. I think that two of the biggest graces, I mean outside Your love, the Father's love and Carsha's love is to have people love me, and admire me, and yet, it doesn't bother me. I just praise and thank God. That's one of the graces...... I can't say it's because I'm humble, Butchie. I can't say that at all. It's just that the Father deals with me in that way. I guess I'm so busy thanking Him when it's over.

But nobody can get into my world, that's the other grace. No one. No, Butchie, You know the secrets of my heart, and that's surely a grace, but no one can faze me. No one at all. It is a grace. A grace from the Father. So it doesn't enter my mind ever. I'm so protected,

Butchie. And I'm protected in this valley......

You're the only one I can talk to like this. Because You already know it, probably. Because we've always been so open..... I know You love me, and I love You so much. All I want to do is have everyone love You, but I want to love You the best. But I want them to love You..... You do? (laughs) You really do? Great.....

I mind it, and I don't. I don't know how to explain it, Butchie. I mind going away, because of the family, and my dogs, and my responsibilities..... But I delight in doing the Father's work.....

It's the sacrifice of leaving the home that the Father uses to make the services so great..... Oh Butchie, I'm fully aware they're great, but I'm fully aware that it's Carsha, the light of Heaven. So there's never pride. It never enters my mind. That's what I said, it's a grace..... No..... Why are You asking me this? Do You have more places for me to go?..... No, I would go. I was just hoping I could have a quiet time in July, but I will go..... Whatever. I feel as though You're planning something for me.....

Well, I planned – but I will do anything You wish – I planned to be quiet. Maybe a retreat, Butchie. Then I go again in August. But whatever You want, it's OK by me. That glint in Your eye makes me nervous. I feel like You have something on the horizon..... I know You want me here, and I want to be here forever.....

No. I've never seen such beauty. I've seen man-made beauty, like at the seminary, but I've never seen anything like this, Butchie, never. There is no comparison.....

I know You love me all the time, and I feel Your love, but when we're together here in the valley, it's so different, it's so special. It's like we cut ourselves away from everyone, and I find deep peace..... I don't know how to express it, but that's a good way. **They are just people that I meet along the way to my Father. To greet them and to love them. To set a good example before them. But not let them tie me down or linger. Because I must go as swiftly as the running deer, as the babbling brook to my Father.....**

I'm not attached, You know that..... I feel free..... No. I'm just amazed at the way You're speaking to me. I love it. I delight in it. I remember once when I was a kid, I saw a picture of Jack Frost. He flew through the air like an angel. Everything he touched glittered. And that's how I feel when You bring me here. You're my Jack Frost and You touch everything with such beauty. Each time it's more beautiful than ever..... *(laughs)* I'm glad You don't mind being compared to him..... I love You too..... A deeper love for You, Butchie, and a deeper love for my Father..... Yes, for Carsha too. I depend upon Him for so much, Butchie. It's in loving Him that I receive the love from You and the Father. There's such fullness of love there.

I still feel I'm on the brink of a new awakening of Carsha..... **I am.....** I feel as though when I love Carsha, Your love and my Father's love is overflowing upon me. I can't quite explain it, Butchie, but even when I call Carsha's name, I feel something within me swelling with love for the Father and for You, my Butchie. I can't quite pinpoint it, but there's something near. Something that You want to reveal to me from my Father, Butchie, about Carsha..... I don't know..... It's like, there can be no love for the Father and the Son unless you have Carsha, the fullness of this love. And if you have Carsha, it's like you have it all wrapped up in a bundle. A priceless treasure that no one can take away from you ever..... I understand that. I can't quite grasp it yet though, Butchie..... I know when You're a serious teacher, there's something You're going to reveal to me, and it blows my mind when You do..... Who said that, the Father?.....

For You, Father..... **This is the hour that there will be an explosion of love for Carsha through Eileen..... An explosion of love wherever I go. The fullness of the love of the Trinity will embrace Your people.** Father, it thrills me to death..... *(laughs)* **To life.** You're funny..... Carsha's so important.....

Father, I want to know so much about it. **In time.....** I want to know so much about it so I can give it to Your children, Father. Oh Father, my soul is so excited over it. It seems as though I won't be able to wait until You give it all to me..... I feel like I'm burning up with love for Carsha, this love that embraces the whole Trinity. I feel that You're going to reveal to me so much, so that I can give it to Your priests..... I don't know how to explain it, Father. I feel like I'm walking toward Carsha in a new, deeper way, and I can feel my soul leap within me, Father..... With all my heart, my Father.

AN EXPLOSION OF LOVE

July 7, 1985

That's very beautiful, Butchie, I wish I could remember the words..... Well, when I go back to my world, I would sing them, and I would think about You even more. They are so precious, I never want them to be lost..... *(laughs)* I don't think anyone knows this side of You. I think they know You're tender and You're loving and You're kind, but I don't think they know how tender and how loving and how kind and how gentle You are..... I'll remember those two lines for sure..... They'll go on and on, over and over, in my mind, and everything else will rush in, in its own place.....

I don't think anyone knows You sing..... *(laughs)* For sure?..... Then I feel privileged..... I don't know about that, but at least I feel privileged..... That is very beautiful..... Well, You certainly do, because I do feel calm and peaceful..... No. I wish I could explain these things to people, but they wouldn't understand it, I don't think. Do You, Butch?..... I wish I could tell them about Your love..... And You're more beautiful than ever, Butchie, even more loving than before..... Sometimes I do get afraid when You look even more loving, as You were this morning. My humanness comes in, and I'm wondering what I'm in for..... *(laughs)* You're funny. But I'm serious..... *(laughs)* I know You are.....

I wish everyone could understand You like this..... But I thought You said Your love was meant for everybody?..... **This is an intimate and special love, and it's meant for me.....** But I want them to know how kind, and how gentle, and how loving You are. How lovable You are in Yourself..... I believe that. I believe everything You say.....

Now, at this moment, I'm just filled with Your love, and yet, I feel like You're going to open a new door, and I don't know what yet, but there is something behind that door..... Yes, I believe it. I believe everything You tell me..... Deeper and deeper in love..... Our love will build the fortress.....

Are You preparing me for my next step?..... Oh, it must have something to do with it..... **You want to shout to the world what it means to be in love with Christ. They'll know there is so much more, and they'll try to pry the secrets from my heart and my soul.** But they will be our secrets? And in this longing to know, they will be deeply moved and touched by grace, Butchie?.....

I wish You could give me another definition of grace..... I feel as though that has something to do with this..... Well, You know, it's a helping aid. That's what we learned..... I wish You could explain it better to me. I understand that much of it..... **It's like a reaching out of Your hand, wanting them to at least touch your fingertips so you can reel them in closer.....** I like that even better..... Reaching out of His hand..... I don't quite understand. I don't like to talk about You up on the cross, Butchie. But I understand what You're saying, that **if You didn't die upon the cross, You wouldn't be able to reach out, because this is the Father's will for us, and grace is the reaching out of the Savior's hand to His people, giving strength, consolation.....**

What else, Butchie?..... **Endurance. All of that comes from grace.** Then the invisible grace is the reaching out of Your hand, helping us to get back..... I know there is so much more, Butchie. Why do You give it to me in dribbles?..... Grace. Grace..... **By the reaching out of Your hand, I was led into my mystical courtship, and I grasped, and I grew and deepened.**

Grace, Butchie, grace. Why do You call it *grace*? What is grace? Why such a word?..... I remember that, the helping aid..... **The helping aid of grace is the reaching out of Your hand. And if the sinner falls, they can be touched by grace, but it's up to us to grasp it..... You love to help.....**

You're giving it to me in dribbles. I can't quite grasp everything, Butchie. I need Carsha to help me. There is a mystery here and I want it to unfold..... Who named it grace? Who named this outreach grace?..... Then why don't we hear more about it?..... It sounds so beautiful. So beautiful..... Certainly no one would reject

Your hand..... I think it's enough. I'll go at any pace You want me to go, Butchie.

I'm just marveling at everything You're saying..... Is it really? Then through me, You'll be reaching out Your hand to these sisters. They'll either accept it, or reject it..... Then through me, You're allowing grace to flow, the outreach of Your hand. I can't quite grasp it yet, Butchie. You better tell Carsha to get busy..... I think I'm on the brink of it, but it's blowing my mind.....

Oh no, no pain, just delight, but it seems so big, so big..... No, I never doubted Your love. You know me better than I know me, and You know I've never doubted Your love. I probably kicked up a storm, but never doubted it..... I'll let it sit. I believe You..... I feel a new depth of love. I can't explain it, Butchie, but I know it's there, and Your face is brighter. I never thought it could be so beautiful, and yet, it's far more beautiful. I know another veil has slipped away, and I feel Your love even deeper, as though it's inside of me, going through channels. And it's so beautiful..... I never want to lose it..... Butchie, see, You tempt me..... I'll remember it, **it's just the beginning.** Just the beginning..... *(laughs)* No, this is just the beginning. It's great.....

I wouldn't have to tell You, Father, I know You can read it in my face..... Even more, Father. Even more..... Yes, I do. I feel as though I'm ready to explode, and yet, I know I won't. It's almost like I will, but I won't..... *(laughs)* Well, I'm glad You understand..... Yes, He did talk about grace. He opened a whole new world of understanding of it..... He said that, Father. **That He'll reach out through me to these sisters**..... He said many were coming out of curiosity, but He will reach out to them..... No, my Father, I never dreamed it was possible to love Him more. I know one could, but I didn't think I could..... I can't explain it, Father, but You know the secrets of my heart, and You know how I feel..... He said that it's the brink of a new awakening. I know a veil has slipped away between us, Father..... That delights me more than ever.....

Sometimes I balk, but You know how much I love You..... He

said Carsha will open the door, and let me see exactly what it is..... He gives the teaching a little at a time, so I won't lose it, Father..... Yes, I am content with that. I just feel as though I'm really loaded with so much love, Father.

I know there is a reason..... That will be beautiful. Then if they see it, they'll have to believe it. Right, Father?..... **There will be an explosion of love for Butchie in my life......** More than ever, my Father, for Carsha..... **They will see it in my preachings, in my words, and then I will withdraw.** Again You say, *withdraw.....* It's the candle, Father. It has gone down lower..... With a single grace I could put it out, Father.

Make it consume faster, Carsha..... **It will be sooner than I think, but in between, there is much work to be done.....** Nope. Whatever You say, Father..... At first I was frightened of it, but now I'm looking forward to going there..... It's almost like being commissioned..... If You say so, Father, **wonderful things will take place**, I believe You. And I know this new outburst of love is just the beginning..... It seems as though, when I look in Your eyes, Father, I see Butchie and Eileen..... Really?..... That's not just because He's here, walking with me?..... That's very beautiful, very beautiful, Father..... I don't want to be an adult and say I'm not worthy, but I feel that unworthiness, Father..... Forever, where no one can ever pry me loose from You. It's where I belong forever, Father.

EILEEN WANTS TO WRITE A BOOK ABOUT HEAVEN

October 13, 1985

This is my favorite spot, Butchie, just sitting here looking over the meadows and the valleys..... I don't know. I think about many things. I think that this all belongs to me and I'll be here forever and I'll never have to leave here again. I'll never get tired. I'll have everything that I love around me.....

I know. I was watching them..... They're the little ones You put in the tree, remember?..... *(laughs)*..... Well I knew You had something, otherwise why would You have Your hand behind Your back? They're very beautiful. You know what's even more beautiful, Butchie? They never die. They'll always be here for me..... It seems as though when I come, You're letting me stay longer..... It seems as though You're revealing more to me about the valley. All the secret nooks and crannies of it..... The flowers look brighter..... The air seems different. Everything seems more alive and more beautiful than ever.....

If I wrote about it, I don't think they'd believe it, Butchie, and yet, I know they're hungry to know about it. But I don't think I could find words to describe it..... You have spoiled me. You've spoiled me in every way..... It's more beautiful than when I was here before, and that's not even hours ago. You have so many secrets and You're beginning to unfold them all before me.....

Look at those flowers. How many times have I been here, Butchie, and I've never seen them before..... I'm just enjoying it..... I get so peaceful I just hate to trot again. I want to stay here all the time..... I know I have work to do..... Not really, Butchie. Sometimes I think for a split second I wish I didn't have a ministry. I would like to withdraw into my own house and stay there. Then I know I'm touching these souls for the Father, and I know the price You paid for them, Butchie, and then I want to do it.....

Nope. I guess that's my Father..... No. I'm fully aware of all those crosses, Butchie..... No, I don't think so. I guess it's because I love

You so much. I guess it's because I love You that much..... I know there is a change coming over me..... It's good. Why would it be bad?..... I'm seeing things differently, Butchie. I don't want those people to think I'm something I'm not. I really want to be good, Butchie. Not to please them, to please You, to please my Father. And Carsha seems to be giving me ever so many lights into things..... Especially You, Butchie, in the Eucharist.....

Yes, He told me about that. How they must look at You, concealing Yourself in this wafer and beg for an increase of faith..... But, Butchie, I see You, and they don't see You. Not as I see You..... Then this is what they must be told..... Butchie, I don't want to leave them out of the valleys. I want them to go as high as they can in the kingdom. And yet, when I'm here, I feel very selfish, like I've told them enough, now You take care of it and let me stay here..... You say that because You love me, but I do feel selfish about it.....

No, Butchie, I don't. It sounds silly because I'm not so bright, but I'm not afraid of them. I think I'd feel more at peace with them than with the charismatic people, like they're my kind of people..... I don't know exactly what I mean. You thought I would be out of place with them because of all the gifts You have given me. I think I'm going to feel more comfortable with them than with the charismatic people. Because they want to be good and I want to be good..... I don't think I'm going to feel out of place with them.....

I really do. I feel as though there is a race to use the gifts and to copy the gifts they haven't got. I think with these people, I'll just feel comfortable being what I want to be. Loving You and loving the Father and Carsha, and they'll accept me for that and there won't be a race for gifts and all that other stuff. Do You agree with me, Butch?..... See, I knew You would understand..... No. Sometimes I don't know how You take us, I don't know how You can stand us, to tell You the truth, Butchie.....

I saw them when I first came. They were very beautiful. They look like nuts, and yet, different than our kind..... Nope. Bigger..... *(laughs)* I've never seen a nut tree here before. See? That's what I mean. You are showing me more and more..... But they're different. Different. They're almost as big as one of our figs. You'd only need one of them for a pot of fudge. You wouldn't need all the little ones. *(laughs)* A whole bag full..... It just seems like the Father outdid Himself here in the kingdom, especially here in the valley.....

Butchie, You know what, I would love to write a book about Heaven..... About the different plateaus. How they would feel content at the plateau at which they arrive. They won't be jealous. Who can visit who, and the others won't mind. I would love to tell them about the beauty and about Your fruits and Your flowers and the lakes and the streams. About the nut tree. About the fishes. About everything paying homage to You, Butchie..... About the *[absence of the force of]* gravity, how everything goes so swiftly across the meadow. How nothing dies and everything lives. How the fruit is so sweet and the flowers smell so good. There is so much I could tell, but I don't know if they would believe me.....

I bet it would be a beautiful book, Butchie, and I bet they'd all want to come to Heaven, and they wouldn't be satisfied with just getting in the door. They would really work hard to get to the seventh place..... See, that too, because I like the cool, clear breeze, and how it kisses my cheeks and whispers as it passes by, *[it's here]* only because I love it..... I could go on and on, Butchie, from everything You have revealed to me, and there is so much more, I know. They would hunger and thirst after You, Butchie. They wouldn't be content staying on earth..... I think it would give them a thirst for You..... I know, but those things pass away. This will never pass away. At times, I feel so selfish that I know so much about the valley, Butchie. I don't mean brain stuff. I mean truth stuff. Real good stuff. Like the kingdom and the valley. I feel selfish because I have so much.....

I could care less about that. I wouldn't care if I was the dumbest person in the whole world as long as I know all this. This is what makes me happy, not that other stuff..... No I wouldn't. I wouldn't trade it for anything..... *(laughs)* No, not even for that. So You better knock it off or the Father is going to be mad at me for contaminating Your thoughts..... Of course I wouldn't care..... No. If He gave me the choice of whatever or coming here, no way would I take that. I would come here as fast as I could..... No..... I hope the Father doesn't hear You..... I don't think I'm silly, I think I'm truthful.....

Getting back to the book, I think it would be the best book in the whole world. They would realize they're just on a journey to real life..... You could call it a journey to real life, Butchie, because that's what it would be. It's like going to the Cape. You know the way. You certainly wouldn't get onto different routes because you haven't reached your destination, the kingdom, Butchie..... I feel privileged, but I feel sad for them because when Carsha allows me to tell them something, they listen so.....

That's only half the stuff I could tell them. I could tell them the feasts and how the table is always set, but doesn't have to rest on the ground. Remember what I did when I first saw the tablecloth? The Father laughed so much. I kept looking under it to see what was holding the tablecloth up. There was nothing there..... *(laughs)* He did. He did. He said, "I get more joy out of watching your face than out of anything that's on this table." I thought it was a real neat trick.

But see, Butchie, they don't know about all this stuff. They don't know the happiness and the joy and the laughter. Some actually think they're going to be bored in the kingdom. They don't realize it's a whole new life of good and no evil, no pain..... Butchie, I could go on and on and on. *(laughs)* I don't think any book could hold it all.....

I think the valley brought it all on because it's so beautiful today, Butchie. It's so beautiful, and the flowers are brighter and everything is more beautiful than ever. And I'm more peaceful than ever and I feel selfish keeping it all to myself..... Yes, but there are other people You have to share with, Butchie. It would be selfish if we kept it to both of ourselves, right?.....

I don't know. It looks like a daisy, but it's far more beautiful.....

Friday? I don't remember that..... Oh, I remember now. I began to cry because of the passion..... Really. That's so beautiful. Only you and the Father could do that..... Lockmeis. Tear drops. Tear drops.....

See what I mean, Butchie?..... There is everything *[here that]* I love, for sure, the animals, the trees and the mountains and the meadows. And everything I love and everything in this valley has a meaning. It hasn't been put here by chance. The Father has a meaning for everything, even the lockmeis. How do you spell that, Butchie?..... Then *e-i* is like two *e's.* Like *me*. Lockme..... It's pronounced me. Like *me*, the person? Lockmeis. They're beautiful.....

It's Butchie, Father. He's showing me the tear drop flowers..... Father, I didn't realize that everything in the valley is mine because it had a meaning for me..... On earth it would be called the passion flower, but we can't use that name here. Right, Father?..... I'll keep running around, Father, looking for the meaning of everything.....

The fishes?..... I used to cry when I used to bring fishes home. They would have hooks in their mouths and I would cry to see their eyes still open..... Really, Father? **That's why You gave me all the different fishes in the the brook. Because I had compassion for them, and it was a likeness of the Father's love.** The same with the little baby animals, because I love them..... It seems like the whole valley has a different meaning for me now. It was always precious and very beautiful, a very special place, but now even more so. And I know it's Carsha, Father, giving me new lights..... **You want me to treasure my valley.** I do treasure it, Father. **Now in my busy world, I must run back to my valley as often as I can, and make new discoveries.....** They're discoveries, Father? Then You're telling me that I'm going to be very busy, and You want me to run here as often as I can to find the peace that only this place can give to me.....

Yes, I know I'm tired, Father. I'm not working any harder. There are just so many other things, but I'll get over it. **This is a very important ministry.** Even more important than I have now, Father? **I must seek the silence and the solitude of my valley because without this I couldn't survive. It's like food for my soul and peace**

for my body..... I'll remember that, Father..... No, I'm enjoying it. I really love it so much, my Father..... I've always been peaceful here, Father, but this is more than ever..... Yes..... **It's very important even when I do the retreat, to retreat myself to my valley, and to be still and enjoy the beauty that *[here]* surrounds me.....** Yes, I remember that, Father..... You said that to me a hundred times. **The devil can use very good people to destroy my peace.....**

I didn't know that, Father, but it's so wonderful to hear You say that..... I remember that..... The white challenger of faith..... Yes, I remember that. I was going to my Priests' Day and I noticed all the junk and mess, and amidst it there was that beautiful, beautiful bouquet of flowers, like orchid and marigold. And You said, **"You will be like a flower. I will lift you up and you will shine before man, amid all the garbage and the turmoil of the world."**.....

I don't quite understand what it means. I trust what You're doing, and I'm sure You know what You're doing. Whatever it is, I'll go along with it, Father..... I know You love me..... I love You so much. I find it harder and harder to leave my valley, Father. It's so beautiful, You should write a book about it, Father..... I don't know if they could believe it or grasp it all.....

I remember that well..... Such suffering and such pain. Is there more? If there is, then open up the door and let me see Your face, let me feel Your lips, let me touch the face of God made man, let me hold Your hand. Oh yes, Father there is so much more. I remember it, Father. Then again You're saying to me, **"Eileen, there is so much more that I want to reveal to you. Spend your time in the valley"**..... I will, Father. I promise You I will.....

That's my greatest joy, when You call me a child of the Father. If I had nothing else, Father, that would fill me.

THE FATHER WANTS HIS PEOPLE TO KNOW THE TRUTH

December 1, 1985

I really never realized that before, Butchie. It feels like a light from Carsha..... Sure it would be a very good Christmas subject, but I need time so Carsha can work in me, Butchie..... Oh yes, **Mary is in pursuit of the child given to her by Jesus Christ on the Cross. The soul is given to her through baptism, and she pursues it.....** Yes, that would be by the grace given by Jesus. Right?..... I never even thought of that before..... I'm sure with Carsha's help it could be a beautiful tape about Mary, to make people aware of how much she loves us.....

Butchie, Carsha gives me so many lights, and I don't have the time..... Well, if He gives me the lights, He should give me the time..... You give me so many ideas. Then I never have time to fulfill them..... I know, but who knows better than You..... No. I promise You I will tomorrow. Some time tomorrow. What is this urgency over it anyhow?..... It's true, they do slip away, but I would love to do one on Mary..... I would love to do that too. It seems as though You're pressing upon my heart all these beautiful inspirations, and I know it's the light of Carsha. I know people would be so interested in that, because I'm interested in it, Butchie.....

I felt that today, when Lassie looked so sick, but not whining or complaining. The moment she felt my hand stroking her, she became alert, and that's how I feel with the Father. When I feel completely wiped out, I feel His hand and I know He's there..... No, Butchie. I just couldn't survive without it..... It's such an eerie feeling, Butchie. I wish I had time to put it all down, but I just don't have time. You're with me all day. You see what my schedule is, and all the monkey wrenches that are thrown into it..... Nope, look at today. Shannon and Mary, Kathy and Neil. Everyone over for the nice quiet dinner Colleen and I were going to have. And it's chaos afterwards, no quiet time at all. They mean well, but it's a constant invasion. No time at all..... I'm not complaining. I love them. The only thing I'm complaining about is, You want me to do tapes, and when can I do them?.....

Yes, maybe I could do that..... This past week, Butchie, You have revealed so much to me, not only about Mary, but about the animals. You revealed so much about Christmas, and Your birth. I don't want to lose it, Butchie. Sometimes I wake up at night, and You know how I think about it, and it's so beautiful. I think the whole world should know about it. We don't hear this, Butchie. This is the part we don't hear..... Well, I think that's why He's allowing it to happen, because He wants them to know about it..... How can I tell them? I can't even get my own thoughts together..... Butchie, You just have to help me in this area. I just can't do it alone..... I want to tell them what You told me this morning, especially about those precious animals..... They don't understand all of that..... And about the hay coming through Your blanket and pinching You. They don't understand that. They just look at You in the manger, that's all. They think it was all hunky-dory. They don't understand everything else.....

But I need time..... No. Remember that rhyme, precious time? That tape on time?..... "It never stands still so I can catch it. It just keeps running and running, and I'm forever pursuing, but never catching"..... Nope, I don't want You to be a contradiction. I know You can't turn it back. But how can I pursue it?..... Yeah, it sounds easy, but it doesn't work for me, ever..... No..... I just felt sorry about last year. It doesn't bother me as much as I'm pretending. What bothers me is that I want everyone to know about it..... See, they don't understand that part either. We see the manger looking so beautiful, we don't know everything..... I know what a lean-to is. It's where the animals get behind a shelter from the wind..... Thank God for the stars. The Father knew they were stirring...... See, that could be a book in itself.....

I don't know, Butchie, what I'm going to do..... Yes, but see, that too is a revelation all of its own. You're giving me too much. I grasp it, and then it goes until I look at the manger or think about it..... But don't You think everyone should know it, or at least think about it?..... Well, You'll have to give me time..... Butchie, You're funny..... Well, fact as it is, it's still funny. Maybe I should play the tape for You on time. I can't grasp it, it flees. It's on the constant go..... I'll do that. If I write it, it won't slip away, it'll come back to me, Butchie..... No..... I'm honored that You're trusting all these secrets to me, Love, but I just need the time to do it. I will write it when I can..... Nope. Well, it's up to You not to let me forget.....

You bring me so much peace, so much love..... At this moment You flood me with peace. Now all the assignments don't seem heavy to me. I just feel so light, almost like floating.....

Yes, I do want to know more about Joseph. We don't know too much about him..... I want to know everything about him, Butchie..... If He will..... Butchie said You would tell me more about Joseph, Father. And I said, "If He will"..... Many things, Father, but mostly about Jesus in the manger..... I really want to get into all of this. I don't want children or people to think it's a story and a myth, because You said it wasn't, Father. I want them to know the truth about the manger, and about Butchie.....

Yes. I want them to know about Adam and Eve, what You have taught me, my Father..... No..... From now until Christmas?..... Christmas Eve, Father?..... **No matter how busy your schedule will be, I will give you two hours. You will use from twelve to two according to your time**..... And You will tell me all these things, my Father?..... **Even more**..... Is there an urgency for this, Father?..... I promise. I know I'm not so good, my Father, in keeping promises. I promise with all my heart I will give this time to You, Father, and to Your teachings..... Who's doing that?..... But Father, how can they get rid of truth? And the birth of Butchie is truth.....

But there's nothing really centered on Adam and Eve..... Yes, I know You say it's truth, and I believe You, Father. I believe everything You say. I don't doubt You at all..... No, why would You want to fool me?..... **You will reveal secrets about the birth of Butchie, and I will write them.** .... No. We'll keep it like a date..... I love You too, Father. It will be a good preparation for the feast..... It will be kept secret until You tell me, Father.....

But who?..... If You say so, Father, just one..... **The more You bring me deeper into Your revelations** *[the more she will be attacked]*..... A combat zone? Father, I don't think I could get into bigger zones than I get into lately. I'm not afraid of that, Father..... **Michael will be with me.....** *(laughs)* He's so funny. He stood right in front of the breakfast table, and all I could see was him. I almost choked on the quiche..... *(laughs)* I didn't know what Michael was up to..... Of course I love him, Father..... Nope. You're the best. Nobody could ever replace the love I hold for You, my Father..... I don't know how to explain it, Father. It's light. It's airy. It's radiant. It's warm. It's just so beautiful..... You know You don't have to ask me that twice. We made a deal..... No. I won't..... No. I promise, my Father..... I'll do everything You said..... No, I'm just dying to find out more, Father. I know there is so much more, so much more..... *(laughs)* You sound like me. I'm teaching You slang, Father..... *(laughs)* No one would believe that You spoke like that.....

UNANSWERED CHRISTMAS QUESTIONS

December 25, 1985

I just love being here. But when You present Yourself as a baby, it's just . . . *[laughs)* Butchie, it's still You, but it seems like Christmas time, the Christmas season..... *(laughs)* No, that's not it. But the sight of You lying there in the hay doesn't remind me of baby Jesus, it reminds me of big Butchie. I know You're one and the same, but it doesn't feel the same..... Yes..... He can see all the stars..... You know the people think it was beautiful. I don't know anybody who would say, "Yech!" But it's so poverty stricken..... No, it doesn't bother me at all.....

There are so many questions that are not answered in Scripture, Butchie..... Some answers I want to know, some I don't care about. Maybe I'll care about them later on. They'll come up in my curiosity, but right now I'm not curious about them..... I believe that. I really don't know if I want to know the answer or not..... If You want to tell me, You can, but it's up to You. It's just so peaceful, I just want to be quiet, and enjoy this peace.....

I'm afraid to let this season go by. I want to get all I can get from this season, or it will be lost to me forever..... I know there is a new year, but what is this feeling I have inside of me, afraid to let go of '85, the Christmas of '85. I think it's more meaningful than ever..... This one means so much more, I don't know why. You've told me so much more this year than ever before, like Joseph with the cheese and the bread. About the water that never ran out.....

I always thought it was a million miles away, but now that You tell me it's not really that far away. But still it was a trip for Mary, right? Being pregnant and all?..... Well I guess two hours on a donkey is far enough. Two hours by foot is far. Two hours would be far enough for me, I'd say..... Don't do that. That straw tickles my nose..... Butchie, stop fooling around. I want You to tell me some more. Take the straw out of Your mouth. You look just like a gangster...... *(laughs)* You are funny. Humphrey Bogart. Do You know about him, the movie gangster? That's who you look like chewing that straw. Knock it off and talk to me some more..... Talk to me..... Everything. Not just one thing. Loads of stuff..... Well, I thank You for that. I'm glad I know more than most people know about it, but I'm still curious about some things..... I know about that..... Sure, that's for starters..... You are so funny. You have a one track mind. I love You too, Butchie, but I want to know these things. I'm not so bright, You know, but if You tell me, I'll remember them forever.....

Scripture doesn't say that. If I say it, they'll say I'm a heretic..... Nope. As long as we know it, that's all I care about. That's what I want to know, Butchie..... I want to know if Mary ever lost sight that You were God, the Son of the Father?..... **Never for a moment, but it never interfered with her correcting You.....** Yes. **She was simple and open and honest, so if You had to be corrected, You were corrected.....** That must have been tough for You because if You were the Son of the Father, how could You stand to be corrected? You don't make mistakes..... See, this is where I'm really puzzled. **In Your humanness You had to take a step at a time, to learn.** *(laughs)* **You had to learn how to walk.....** It's kind of hard for me to grasp it all..... I understand obedience, but didn't You ever forget and say, "Hey Joseph, this is better, this is the better way."..... **Jewish children were very obedient and submissive.** Well, there must have been some naughty kids around?..... **Not as a whole.....**

I want to know about the Magi, Butchie. Did they really come? Did they really give You these gifts? I'm not doubting it, but I hear so many different things about it..... I know. But did they go back and talk about it to their people? They came from far off lands, and they followed the star. Didn't they go home and talk about it? Didn't that help to convert the world?..... Who could keep such a secret?..... That's what I wanted to ask You, about Herod..... *(laughs)* No..... Why did he do all this?..... Yes, that's what I mean *[the massacre of the innocent babes]*..... Oh, so that's why..... But all the experts didn't agree about the time *[of the birth of the Messiah. Apparently Eileen is repeating Jesus' explanation why Herod chose to kill all the infants under two years of age]*..... But they did see the star?..... Many scientists, doctors, everyone, they don't agree on anything sometimes..... I think I understand as much as You want me to understand. Butchie, why wasn't all of this written?..... **Revelations are still coming on and on.** *[See note at end of next page}* And it will be? Until when?..... *(laughs)* No. Come on. I want to hear some more..... **There is nothing more important than that** *[than what is written in Scripture?]*. But I like to know what is going on in between..... *(laughs)* No. For my own use, Butchie, just for me. When You love someone as much as I love You, I want to know about You..... I want to know the suffering You went through. I want to know some of the joyful things that happened in Your path that's not written..... No, I think it was the most beautiful Christmas ever. I'm just afraid of losing it. I don't want to see the new year come yet. I want to hang on to '85 as long as I can..... I hope that's right. If You say it, I'm sure it is.

Sometimes I don't feel like I'm falling deeper in love with You, Butchie. Sometimes I feel like I'm being pulled away. We don't have so much time together..... I do look over and I see You. It seems as though the only time I have is when I go to bed at night..... But I miss that time..... I think that's why we have drawn ever so close during this Christmas. I don't want it to end. I'm afraid of what begins in the new year..... No. No. I longed for the old house and the quietness I had there, the time we had together..... I don't know if I like that..... I have to think about it..... I like that part of it..... I remember that story, the three little pigs. "And he huffed and he puffed and he blew the house down." But then that was made of solid brick, and the wolf couldn't blow it down..... Somehow our love is even more solid. Nothing can ever tear it down. And they can huff and they can puff and they can blow, but it will never fall down..... **It's in the yearning and the craving for the silence that blows it ever so strongly and blows it so firmly..... Having the time is the consolation. To keep yearning for it is the cross and the**

strength..... I buy that, but I don't know if I like it too much..... I love the Father..... Well, I do love His Son..... It's comfortable *[straw as a bed for the Infant]*, but I can feel it tickling me. It must have hurt you some..... We stick together, right?.....

I don't know if I know that stillness, Butchie. But I've known another stillness when You brought me to the manger. It was an awesome quietness, a different kind of stillness.

Note: God is not limited in His capacity to impart revelations for the sanctification of persons, and the upbuilding of His Church. The Catechism of the Catholic Church *states:* "Throughout the ages there have been so-called 'private revelations,' some of which have been recognized by the authority of the Church." [67] *See also the* Introduction.

ON THE EVE OF EILEEN'S MISSION TO KOREA

April 23, 1986

Well, Butchie's always full of surprises, but this is one of the biggest yet..... I had not the slightest intimation..... They're so beautiful, Father..... They're all beautiful. I can't say which is the most beautiful, one's more beautiful than the next..... *(laughs) I* don't know. It looks like a berry wine. I get amazed at the glasses, if that's what You call them, Father..... Well, I don't think they could stand the dishwasher. Nor would I want to put them there.....

I can hear them, they're so beautiful..... You know, if I heard a violin *[at so high a pitch]*, I would hold my ears at the screech, even if it was beautiful. But this is more beautiful than ever, my Father..... I'm glad You did..... Oh no, it's just because I know there are three more *[orders of angels]*, and I'd like to have them present, my Father. In anything like this, I always look for them..... Yes, I remember. There are the cyclins, the archlins, and the trialins..... *(laughs)* I remembered them all..... They have two names, right?..... Archlins. Right, my Father?..... But I don't understand why You have all of this. It's not my birthday..... It wouldn't be a party, would it?..... But tell me what is it all about?..... **The Father's word is going into a new world**..... But why today, my Father, I still have time..... *(laughs)* That's for sure, too much interference.....

But Your word is there, Father..... Thank You, that makes me feel good. That gives me a little bit of assurance, I don't know how much..... What is it, my Father?..... It's so beautiful, I'm afraid to spoil it by opening it..... I will..... *(long pause)* **I bring to You a gift. An assurance of my love. A gentleness that only I am permitted to give thee. A radiance that will draw them to you. They may not understand everything you say, but the gentleness of Mary will bring them into the Father's heart. This is my gift for you, Child......**

But Mary, where are those words coming from. I hear them. I feel them. They're not in the box..... Oh, I know, Carsha. But I see Him, and I don't see Him..... I don't know what to say..... Thank

You, my Mother. I couldn't dream of a gift like that in a million years..... *(laughs)* **Nor could you.** Then how did you do it? **Through Carsha.....** Oh Mary, Oh Mother, you're always the humblest..... *(laughs)* And so honest, **you couldn't dream of it either, without Carsha.....** Yes, Butchie...... **Enduring love.** Enduring love. Enduring love. Even when I'm tired, I worry about them not understanding me..... Enduring love. Thank You so much, Butchie..... I don't know why You're waiting until after the others, but I'll go along with that, and the Father..... And You, Carsha..... Yes, I'm always talking about the furnace of burning love..... *(long pause)* Will that really happen, Carsha?..... That is so beautiful. I've always wanted to do that..... That it could happen to others. Never dreaming it could really, really happen to me..... **You** ***[will place]*** **on my heart such a fire of burning love, that when I speak to my Father's children, each word will be a flame leaping out of my furnace of love, and enkindling all of their hearts, and they'll be on fire with the deepest love they have ever experienced.....** Carsha, that's so beautiful. Between Butchie's enduring love, and my Mother's gentleness, and this furnace, how can I lose?.....

(laughs) Yes, Father. I can tell by that twinkle in Your eye that there's so much more..... **You have blessed me with wisdom and knowledge to call all the greatest healings. And they will know that it is not I, but my Father working through me. They will see the power of Almighty God coming from a mother, a wife, a grandmother, and they will be stunned and amazed, and they'll cry out to each other, "It's truly God visiting His people.....** I don't know what to say, my Father.....

Yes, I have been worrying about it, because of the lack of communication, Father. You just can't say things the way you would say them in English.... Yes, they loved me..... I trust everything You say is true..... *(laughs)* Thomasino, I don't know what else You could give me..... You'll have to slow down, because they're all coming at once. I can't seem to grasp it all. Sometimes, Thomas, you forget who you're dealing with..... *(laughs)* It's still dopey me..... **I will not**

back down. I will have the strength of the written word..... I don't know, I'm overwhelmed. I'm excited to begin, and just overwhelmed that you would care so much for me..... Yes, Thomas, I did. I worried about the baggage, the luggage and the clothes. I never dreamed you would give me all these spiritual things to carry.....

Catherine..... What?..... Beautiful. **If I wore but one outfit, I'd have everything I need. Nothing else is important.....** We won't drink to that..... Butchie. You make the toast..... I don't have to repeat, Butchie, I can just listen..... All right....**I toast to each and every one of you, my bride, Eileen, my Slug. We'll be on our honeymoon, when we will draw so close to each other, where the world cannot enter, man cannot drift in. We will isolate ourselves and fade into each other, and we will open the door to another world, and with us we will bring our Father in a new and different way. Now you all toast to this.** Butchie. My Butchie..... *(laughs)* I think one toast is enough, it is more than I can handle. Yes, my Father. But how can I fail? No way..... **I will be Your rainbow, Father, Your covenant into a new world..... You will have peace and joy and love. And I will not be known as the American, I will be known as the daughter of my Father** *(long pause)*..... And the angels sing. It is so beautiful..... Yes, I love You, Father. I'll always love You..... The voices seem to be fading, and yet, the tone is so beautiful.

INTERVIEW

What happened?
Nothing. We were at a party.
What was the reason for the party?
Going to Korea.
A goodbye party?
A celebration party. They all had gifts to give me.

EPILOGUE

This concludes the three book series *Conversations in Heaven.* This third book ends prior to Eileen's first mission to the Republic of Korea in 1986. This was followed by mission's in 1989 and 1993. Her work in Korea in 1986 and 1989 is recounted in two chapters of her first book *Eileen George: Beacon of God's Love: Her Teaching.*

The effect these missions had is indicated by the following words of Stephen Cardinal Kim, Archbishop of Seoul. They will be a fitting conclusion to this trilogy. They were written as a preface to the translation into Korean of Eileen's first book in September 1993, just prior to Eileen's third visit to Korea and were included in *Conversations in Heaven II* with Cardinal Kim's gracious permission.

I would like to simply introduce Mrs. Eileen George to you... This woman loves God the Father very, very much and wishes to share with people all over the world the knowledge of God's love.

Eileen George has been to our country twice, and it makes me happy to think she will visit us now a third time.

In 1989 Eileen shared her teaching with priests, brothers and sisters numbering 80,000. From her whole heart and soul she gave to many God the Father's love, peace and joy. In seeing Eileen George we see what can happen to us ordinary people, too. We should feel moved to rise above ourselves to wholehearted self-giving.

At this time it is my hopeful wish for all Korean Christians, that, as we gladly meet and receive Eileen's spiritual teaching, we will allow that teaching to make a big change in our Faith-life.

INDEX

F

J

K

L

M

N

O

P

Q

R

S

T

Other Eileen George Books

Eileen George: Beacon of God's Love: Her Teaching

Eileen George's Conversations in Heaven I

Dialogues with Jesus and God the Father

Eileen George's Conversations in Heaven II

Each book in the *Conversations in Heaven* series is $10 plus $2.50 for shipping and handling. For additional books the shipping and handling charge is $1.50 each.
For videotapes and audio tapes: write for catalogue

Order from

Meet-The-Father Ministry, Inc.
363 Greenwood Street
Millbury, Mass 01527

The Meet-The-Father Ministry is a tax exempt foundation whose purpose is to perpetuate Eileen George's teaching